Some Achieve Greatness

Lessons On Leadership From Shakespeare And One Of His Greatest Admirers

John Bell

16pt

PANTERA PRESS

The information in this book is published in good faith and for general information purposes only. Although the author and publisher believe at the time of going to press that the information is correct, they do not assume and hereby disclaim any liability to any party for any loss, damage or disruption caused by errors or omissions, whether they result from negligence, accident or any other cause.

First published in 2021 by Pantera Press Pty Limited
www.PanteraPress.com

Text copyright © John Bell, 2021
John Bell has asserted his moral rights to be identified as the author of this work.

Design and typography copyright © Pantera Press Pty Limited, 2021
® Pantera Press, three-slashes colophon device, and *sparking imagination, conversation & change* are registered trademarks of Pantera Press Pty Limited. Lost the Plot is a trademark of Pantera Press Pty Limited.

This work is copyright, and all rights are reserved. Apart from any use permitted under copyright legislation, no part may be reproduced or transmitted in any form or by any means, nor may any other exclusive right be exercised, without the publisher's prior permission in writing. We welcome your support of the author's rights, so please only buy authorised editions.

Please send all permission queries to:
Pantera Press, P.O. Box 1989, Neutral Bay, NSW, Australia 2089 or info@PanteraPress.com

A Cataloguing-in-Publication entry for this book is available from the National Library of Australia.

Cover Design: Evi O
Publisher: Lex Hirst
Editor: Alexandra Payne
Proofreader: Tom Langshaw
Illustrations: Cathy Wilcox
Typesetting: Kirby Jones
Author photo: Naomi Hamilton Photography
Printed and bound in Australia by McPherson's Printing Group

TABLE OF CONTENTS

INTRODUCTION	iv
THE IDEAL LEADER	1
COURAGE, OR HOW TO BE A LEADER IN TIMES OF CRISIS	13
DECISIVENESS, TIMING AND TOUGH DECISIONS	38
ARROGANCE	58
ENTITLEMENT	80
AMBITION	93
CHARISMA, CONFIDENCE AND HUMILITY	110
INTEGRITY AND HUMANITY	124
AFTERWORD	145
ACKNOWLEDGEMENTS	148
BACK COVER MATERIAL	152

Some are born great, some achieve greatness and some have greatness thrust upon 'em.
William Shakespeare, *Twelfth Night*

That some achieve greatness, is proof to all that others can achieve it as well.
Abraham Lincoln

SHAKESPEARE ON INTEGRITY

This above all: to thine own self be true,
And it must follow, as the night the day,
Thou canst not then be false to any man.
Hamlet

INTRODUCTION

Leadership is not a person or a position. It is a process and a complex moral relationship that ought to be based on trust, obligation, commitment, emotion and a shared vision of the good.
Joanne B. Ciulla

For the last twenty years or more the cry on everybody's lips has been 'Leadership!' Around the globe people have been yelling about it, demanding it, begging for it. From the farcical spectacle of short-lived Australian prime ministers shoving each other through the revolving door, scandalous failures of governance in Australia's financial institutions and the Australian Defence Force, and the moral abyss in church leadership, to the mess of Brexit and the after-effects of the chaotic Trump administration, stable, reliable, sensible leadership has been in short supply.

Then in early 2020 the world faced its greatest leadership challenge since World War II: COVID-19 hit the planet Earth like a meteor and, before we could blink, had become a pandemic. World leaders reacted in ways that would define each of them, some surprisingly, some not. Most European heads of state reacted strongly but too slowly. The most inept leaders like Trump and Brazil's Bolsonaro went straight to their default positions of denial, cover-up and misinformation, with catastrophic outcomes for their populations and economies. China, the supposed source of the virus, struck a posture of outraged innocence.

Amazingly, Australia, whose politics over the last couple of decades has been defined by ugly and juvenile infighting, responded in a way that could serve as a model to the rest of the world. Prime Minister Scott Morrison proclaimed a pandemic way ahead of the World Health Organization and we saw a novel and extremely welcome bipartisan response across the Commonwealth. State premiers handled the lockdown, social distancing, self-isolation and a gradual easing of restrictions firmly, each according to local conditions. Expert advice from the medical fraternity was sought, accepted and acted on. The public was kept well informed as to what was happening and why. And they responded, for the most part, with generosity and a sense of pride in their social cohesion. New Zealand, strongly led by Jacinda Ardern, was similarly successful.

As I write this, in late 2020, the pandemic is far from over and every country, including Australia, is on the alert for further waves of infection. But so far the whole episode has proved to be a reassuring example of what decisive, sensible and inclusive leadership can achieve, not only at the top, but all the way down the line. You don't have to be a prime minister to be a leader. You might be a local fire chief, school principal or manager at a McDonald's outlet.

Reaching for hyperbole to describe seismic events, the media often resort to the word 'Shakespearean'. And indeed we can learn a lot from William Shakespeare (1564–1616) about leadership – good and bad. Besides being a genius whose mind could encompass great vistas of the imagination, he had an acute sense of historical perspective and an uncanny psychological intuition that enabled him to look deep into people's innermost beings and to do it with wit, empathy and a complete lack of sentimentality.

His career as an actor and dramatist meant he spent every waking moment observing and analysing people's behaviour and rendering it on a public stage before a critical, discriminating and highly sophisticated audience. As head of the theatrical troupe favoured by Queen Elizabeth and King James, he spent a lot of time close to the seat of power, with an opportunity to observe all the facets of leadership that determined the day-to-day government of sixteenth- and seventeenth-century England.

It was a dangerous time for any artist to be openly critical of the hierarchy, but the public theatre earned its popularity by being risky. Shakespeare's plays may be regarded at one level as fables about leadership, often set in a distant location (ancient Rome, Egypt or medieval England) to escape censorship.

It is ironic that this male-centric world should be so identified with one of history's most famous leaders – Elizabeth I, Gloriana (1533–1603). Her leadership attributes were formidable: equipped with a brilliant intellect, a sharp wit, a thorough and multi-lingual education, charm, guile, ambition, a talent for diplomacy and strategic thinking, and a toughness that could be ruthless but could also show moderation, she dominated the era through sheer force of will and the determination to stay in charge. She was never going to submit to a man whom she must swear to honour and obey. Her title 'the Virgin Queen' was her declaration of independence.

One of her great displays of leadership was her handling of the attempted invasion of England by the Spanish Armada of 1588. Warned by her counsellors that she should take refuge in London, she rode instead to Tilbury and addressed her troops:

> I am come amongst you ... to live and die amongst you all; to lay down for my God, and for my kingdom, and my people, my honour and my blood, even in the dust. I know I have the body of a weak and feeble woman; but I have the heart and stomach of a king, and of a king of England too!

Surely Shakespeare must have drawn a lot of inspiration from this remarkable woman. He performed for her often as the leading actor and playwright of her personal theatre troupe, the Queen's Men. Her free and audacious spirit may be detected in his characters like Portia and Cleopatra.

It is notable that in Shakespeare's Tragedies and Histories we move in a world where the rules are set by men, and women have to accommodate themselves as best they can. It is in his Comedies where women come into their own, show up men's faults, run rings around them in terms of wit and strategy, and often teach them valuable life lessons.

Shakespeare, as a young man and a young writer, strove to give women a voice – because he believed it would make the theatre more dynamic and because he had a natural sense of justice and sympathy for all those who were marginalised, persecuted and discriminated against.

Inevitably, though, this book deals mainly with male protagonists. Shakespeare lived in a world dominated by men. Its statesmen, soldiers, explorers, educationalists and lawmakers were men. Some remarkable women devoted themselves to intellectual pursuits and the arts, but, unless they bore the privilege of class, they were actively discouraged or at best ignored.

***

I fell in love with Shakespeare in high school, thanks to the enthusiasm of two fine English teachers and an urge to act: I just wanted to get on stage and say those wonderful words. But I was an unlikely performer – a shy loner with a crippling stutter. I was determined to beat the stutter and little by little I did, through sheer perseverance and many stumbles.

I spent much of my four years at Sydney University acting in student productions. Upon graduating I joined Sydney's Old Tote Company in 1963 where I played Hamlet at the age of twenty-two. The following year I played Henry V in a circus tent for the Adelaide Festival.

Then I thought: 'I've peaked ... and I've never had an acting lesson. Where do I go from here?'

Luckily I was given a scholarship by the British Council that took me to England. I joined the Royal Shakespeare Company and that's where

I learned my craft: working day and night for five years with the best of the best.

Coming back to Australia in 1970 I was fired with the idea of creating new Australian plays and staging the classics with an Australian perspective – making them our own.

My first company was the Nimrod, which I co-founded with Ken Horler and Richard Wherrett, and ran, along with several different partners, for the next fourteen years.

We started small, in an old disused stable in Nimrod Street, Kings Cross. It's still there, only now it's called the Stables Theatre, home to the Griffin Theatre Company. Back in 1970 it was a dump, full of junk and old cars. But we took a lease, scrubbed it out and passed the hat around among our mates to raise enough money to put a show on. Ken, a barrister and an old mate from university days, and his wife Lilian drove the fundraising and jumped the legal hurdles.

We opened for business in December 1970, but after our first show the city council closed us down. We had only one toilet for 120 people and there was no fire escape – just a sign over an upstairs window saying: 'In case of fire, jump.'

So we set about putting in more toilets and a proper fire exit, passed the hat around a few more times and reopened a month later. Our repertoire was new Australian plays and innovative productions of the classics, especially Shakespeare. The team was mean and lean. We had a sense of camaraderie, of all mucking in together. We were all equally responsible for every decision that had to be made, be it artistic, financial or strategic.

Within three years we had outgrown the Stables, so we acquired a larger venue in Belvoir Street, Surry Hills. It was the old Fountain Tomato Sauce and Cerebos Salt factory. It's now the Belvoir Street Theatre. We renovated it and enlarged our repertoire, our audiences and our staff.

And now the trouble began. We tried to run the company on democratic lines, seeking ideas and input from everyone in the organisation. This had worked well when we were a small outfit. But now we had become large and successful, and everyone wanted a bit of it. Special interest groups formed with particular agendas they wanted to push in terms of the company's philosophy and management.

All of this was acceptable to a point, but I, my colleagues and the board of directors had left ourselves vulnerable to the perception that everybody's voice was of equal authority – from the chairman of the board to the cleaner, the ushers and the box office staff. People with no experience or understanding of management felt entitled to call the shots. It turned into an Alice-in-Wonderland nightmare, reaching its apogee when, at a company meeting, someone tried to move a motion that it was 'elitist' to *sell* tickets and all tickets should be free. This was democratic socialism gone crazy. It all ended in tears – people left, the place floundered, before it finally reconstituted itself. But the experience taught me you can be democratic only to a point.

What people actually want and need in an organisation is a sound structure with clearly defined roles, each with its own authority and responsibility, benignly headed by a strong CEO and board of directors. People want to know where they sit and are happy to play that role as long as they have a reasonable degree of autonomy and know they will always be listened to when they want to speak.

Naturally, the larger organisations grow the more siloed individuals become, potentially less committed to the overarching goal. They need constant reminding of the company's vision and how they can contribute to it. I speculate as to how much harder this will become as more people work from home, with perhaps little connection with their fellow workers and less feeling of belonging to a family with a particular ethos, raison d'être and set of values.

Having run the Nimrod for fourteen years I was burnt out with the effort of continual fundraising and trying to develop six new plays a year while attracting a healthy box office. I handed over the company to a successor and spent a few years freelancing as an actor and director.

I swore I'd never run another theatre company.

But then in 1990 I was approached by another old friend from university days, the late Anthony (Tony) Gilbert. Tony said he had some money put aside that he'd like to use to promote Shakespeare. Should he set up a foundation or a scholarship? I said: 'What you should probably set up is a theatre company.' Tony handed me the money and said: 'Okay, it's all yours – get on with it.'

The money wasn't enough to actually set up the business, but it was enough for me to go to the Australian Elizabethan Theatre Trust and say: 'Here is some seeding money to set up a company – can you help?' They gave me an office, a telephone and a mailing list and I set about raising funds, with many business lunches, much knocking on boardroom doors and a lot of schmoozing. Within nine months we had raised about three quarters of a million dollars. It wasn't really enough, but I was impatient to get the show on the road and we launched our first Bell Shakespeare season in January 1991.

We couldn't get a theatre, so we hired a circus tent from Circus Oz. It seems crazy, but in the middle of a recession Bell Shakespeare was set up as a national touring company taking large-scale productions of Shakespeare all over Australia, even to the most remote corners, tied in with an extensive education programme, performing in schools and outback communities.

The first eight years or so were the toughest, as we had little government support and few corporate sponsors. We depended on ticket sales and private donors, as well as the dedicated Tony Gilbert, who ploughed a lot of his private fortune into keeping the company afloat.

By 2015, its twenty-fifth year, Bell Shakespeare had established itself as a major performing arts company that had performed to over three and a half million people. It was mounting three productions a year, touring to over thirty venues in all states and territories. The education programme was reaching 80,000 students a year, with another 70,000 online. We were doing important work with Indigenous communities and juvenile justice facilities. And we had enhanced the careers of hundreds of actors, directors, designers, composers and other theatre workers. We had given scholarships to dozens of teachers and students to come and work with us in the rehearsal room and we had commissioned new plays by Australian playwrights.

The company was in sound financial shape with healthy reserves and looking forward to moving into a new permanent home on Sydney Harbour by 2021.

And yet we had been through various crises in those twenty-five years and all of them taught me much – about management, about leadership and about life. I found myself asked more and more frequently to address conferences, conventions and boardrooms on the topic of leadership. So, rather than rely solely on my own experience, I drew on my wellspring of inspiration: William Shakespeare. His worldly wisdom, humanity, compassion and experience in working so close to the seat of power, the English Crown, and hence his understanding of political machinery, charge his plays with a timeless relevance.

The response to those talks encouraged me to write this book, in the hope that it may be of use to those trying to puzzle out what makes a good leader. From courage and decisiveness to ambition, entitlement and integrity, I delve into leadership traits to foster – and pitfalls to avoid.

Good management is crucial to any organisation, but good leaders do more than just manage – they inspire us. And forget the bully-boys, the bombastic showmen who fake their way to the top through lies and cunning to play on people's worst instincts. History is littered with them.

True leadership, as Shakespeare demonstrates again and again, is a quality that entices us to be better and braver than we ever thought we could be, and to create a world that is better than we could have imagined.

***

I stepped down from Bell Shakespeare Company at the end of 2015, considering that more than two decades was quite enough. I felt I'd achieved pretty well everything I'd set out to do and if I stayed on I'd just be repeating myself – and there isn't any artistic satisfaction in that.

It was an incredible experience. I'm grateful for the opportunities I've had and grateful for the mistakes I've made. From these, I have learned:

- Don't be afraid of failure – how else do you learn?

- Seek feedback — both positive and negative. (The latter is more useful.)
- Anticipate failure and how you will manage it.
- Hold constructive post-mortems. See where you went wrong.
- Failure is a better judge of character than success.
- Maintain your passion for the job. People will be inspired by it and want to come along for the ride.
- A dose of self-doubt is healthy; admit it, but don't let it overwhelm you.
- Cultivate your strengths and compensate for your weaknesses by appointing people you trust.
- Trust is essential to any worthwhile lasting collaboration.
- Autocracy can work but only in the short term. Teamwork is more mutually satisfying.
- Affability is a great quality in a leader. No one wants to work for a boss who is grouchy, sarcastic, pessimistic or remote. It's a great asset if people actually enjoy working with you.
- Collaboration brings a valuable variety of perspectives, experience and skills.
- Don't shy away from competition; encourage it. Be responsible for the next generation.

- Always try to work with people who are better than yourself; that's how you learn. Don't listen to the person who has the answers. Listen to the person who has the questions.
Albert Einstein

SHAKESPEARE ON ASPIRATION

We know what we are, but know not what we may be.
Hamlet

Qualities of a Leader

- brains
- wit
- charm
- guile
- diplomacy
- big hair
- whacking stick
- fancy headrest
- frilly neck-brace
- ermine
- structurally-engineered dress
- cojones
- ball skills
- pointy shoes

Wilcox

THE IDEAL LEADER

Things do not happen. They are made to happen.
John F. Kennedy

Did Shakespeare have an ideal leader? His King Henry V displays many of the qualities we acquaint with great leadership. Henry's ambition, energy, charisma, courage, powerful oratory and unabashed jingoism appealed to an Elizabethan population on the verge of Empire and on a constant war footing with France and Spain.

But Shakespeare's innate scepticism and sense of irony meant he displayed the negative side of the ledger as well. Henry's reasons for declaring war on France are a flimsy excuse. The church is bullied into giving its blessing for the war and there is scant regard for loss of lives and treasure. Henry's slaughter of prisoners could rank as a war crime and there is a poignant description of the havoc wrought by soldiers on the French countryside and peasantry.

It is instructive to draw a comparison with Abraham Lincoln, who was notable for his unwillingness to prosecute soldiers' misdemeanours. He kept warrants for execution marked 'Cowardice in the face of the enemy' in his office desk, saying to his officers:

I put it to you, and I leave you to decide for yourself: If Almighty God gives a man a pair of cowardly legs, how can he help their running away with him?

It would be easy to say: 'Oh well, that just goes to show we have become more civilised between the fifteenth and the nineteenth centuries.' But that is not so. Punitive orders far more cruel than those of Henry V have been issued by commanders in wars since then, including wars that are happening around us right now. Think of the Nazi atrocities in Europe, or those committed in Korea, Vietnam, Sarajevo and Syria to name a few. Lincoln was the exception as a commander in chief. He considered pettiness, vengeance and spite to be beneath the dignity of a leader. He knew that compassion and mercy would win him more support than would vindictiveness.

Henry's mighty conquest is followed by a brief epilogue where Shakespeare reminds us that Henry died shortly afterwards and his French territory was reclaimed by Joan of Arc. England collapsed into the devastating civil war known as the Wars of the Roses, which raged from 1455 to 1487 between two rival factions of the royal family – the Houses of York and Lancaster (the Yorkists sported a white rose as their emblem, the Lancastrians a red one). So, in a sense, it was all for nothing. What price glory?

Maybe we are deluding ourselves to pin all our hopes for ideal leadership on one person, at least for the long haul. We are all frail. But maybe we can find inspiration in the man himself. What qualities of leadership did Shakespeare display?

He started out as a middle-class boy from a prosperous country town. His father, John, was a successful dealer in wool, fancy gloves and leather goods, and was for a time the high bailiff of Stratford-on-Avon, which meant his four sons received a free education at one of the best grammar schools in the country. All the tutors were from nearby Oxford.

A hasty marriage at eighteen prevented William going to university; only bachelors were eligible (hence Bachelor of Arts, Bachelor of Science and so on). He could have carried on his father's solid business but was entranced by the theatre and took off to London, acting and writing for companies such as the Admiral's Men and the Lord Chamberlain's Men. A pub theatre culture was emerging in places like the Red Bull and the Boar's Head. But then Shakespeare and a few mates ganged together, formed a company and built their own theatre, the Globe – a wildly ambitious but successful undertaking. So far he exhibits ambition, opportunism and the daring of an entrepreneur.

When they lost the lease on the land on which the Globe stood, Shakespeare's team refused to lose their precious theatre; they simply dismantled it, transported it plank by plank across the Thames and re-erected it on the other side. When the Globe burned down (due to the misfiring of a stage cannon) they rebuilt it, bigger and better than before. In this he displayed a fair degree of cheek and bravado.

As a dramatist he was the great innovator, breaking conventions, discarding old traditions and coining hundreds of new words and expressions. Most playwrights confined themselves to one genre, but Shakespeare embraced the lot – bawdy farces, sexy comedies, historical sagas of Greece, Rome and medieval England, profound tragedies and mystical fairytales. Nothing was outside his scope or his daring. And he created all these wonders on a bare stage in broad daylight, unaided by technical wizardry, relying on a handful of brilliant actors and the greatest dramatic poetry the world has ever heard. He transformed the nature of theatre.

And he kept pushing the boundaries – educating his audience and demanding more and more of them. The trajectory from a knockabout farce like *The Comedy of Errors* to a dark, knotty, complex play like *Measure for Measure* or *Troilus and Cressida*, let alone *King Lear*, is utterly extraordinary.

As a creative artist he was a great listener and observer, and developed a deep and genuine empathy with people from all walks of life. He was tremendously curious and a great researcher, as fascinated by the newest science, technology and exploration as he was by history, classic art and literature.

But in spite of all his acquired erudition and profound insights into human nature, his work maintained a playfulness and a sense of humour – sometimes a bitter and ironic one.

From the start Shakespeare was a collaborator, never a one-man band.

Even as he became the most famous playwright of his generation he kept performing, acting in the daytime and writing new plays at night. He directed his own productions and helped run the business. Because women were not allowed on stage, he hired and trained the best boy actors and wrote for them the greatest female roles since the days of ancient Greece. He was always part of the team while leading from the front. But nor did he hog the limelight. He saw that Richard Burbage was the greatest actor of his day and wrote for him the roles of Hamlet, Macbeth, Othello, Richard III and King

Lear among others. Has any other actor ever been given such a gift?!

Originality can be a hallmark of successful leadership. You don't have to be a genius to be an original thinker. What you need is the keen eye to spot a potential opportunity and the knack of doing with it something no one else had thought of.

Shakespeare was a great original. Some people say, 'Oh, but he pinched all his stories from other people.' And that's partly true. Just as today we flock along to rehashes of movies about Robin Hood, Ned Kelly or the *Titanic*, Elizabethan audiences enjoyed new versions of stories they already knew. Shakespeare's first job as a hired hand was to patch up and rework plays that had fallen out of date. So he fossicked around and found old plays about King Lear, Hamlet, Henry V and Richard III and completely overhauled them, giving them new layers of meaning and psychological depth expressed in his own matchless poetry. He could turn a musty old melodrama into a profound and timeless tragedy.

He quickly developed his own style as a playwright, gave up collaborating with other dramatists and struck out on his own. He was the first playwright to have his name not only on the front page but also above the title. His name on a show spelled good box office.

In todays worlds of business, science and technology, the leaders are the people constantly on the lookout for a great idea and with the nous to pick it up and run with it. They need to have the courage of their convictions and the ability to persuade everyone else to climb on board.

Shakespeare was dedicated to his craft and a phenomenally hard worker, sometimes turning out four plays a year – an extraordinary achievement given that they were all masterpieces.

He was also remarkably resilient given the vicissitudes of fortune. The plague was a constant threat in London, recurring every few years, during which time all the theatres were closed. The Puritan faction in government clamoured incessantly for plays to be banned, as they were seen as repositories of vice and sedition. (Eventually they had their way, and under the rule of Oliver Cromwell all of London's theatres were pulled down.) Despite these setbacks Shakespeare and his company soldiered on. They were recognised as England's top theatrical troupe when Queen Elizabeth herself adopted them as the Queen's Men – her own private theatre company. After her death they were taken up by her successor, James I, and became the King's Men, performing regularly at court with as many as thirteen of Shakespeare's plays being presented over one Christmas holiday season alone.

When it came to professionalism Shakespeare was no airy dreamer, but balanced art and business with a cool pragmatism. He bought property in London and Stratford and set himself up well for his retirement. He was a realist.

While never displaying arrogance he knew his own worth. As he wrote in one of his sonnets:

> Not marble nor the gilded monuments
> Of princes shall outlive this powerful rhyme.

In his private life he seems to have been regarded by his contemporaries as a modest figure who kept himself in the background, listening and observing. 'Gentle Shakespeare' and 'sweet Mr Shakespeare' were among the epithets bestowed on him.

But the greatest praise of all came from his rival, dramatist Ben Jonson, who hailed him as: 'Soul of the Age! The applause! delight! and wonder of our stage!'

So to briefly summarise, I suggest that Shakespeare displayed the following qualities of leadership:

- At an early age he decided on a life course and stuck to it with tenacity.
- He was ambitious, a risk-taker and a visionary.
- He was a great innovator who broke boundaries and redefined his art form.
- He was versatile and quick to adapt to changing circumstances.
- He was endlessly curious about a wide range of topics, which fed into his art.
- He didn't take himself too seriously and retained a sense of playfulness.
- He was a great collaborator, never top dog but one of the team.
- He sought out and nurtured a fresh generation of talent.
- His originality was in spotting potential material and turning dross into gold.
- He was dedicated to his profession, with a resilience that refused to accept defeat.

Some people say, 'We don't know much about Shakespeare.' On the contrary, I think we know pretty much everything about him: everything he saw, heard, thought, felt and loved.

But of course the man was an actor, a fabulist; and it's very hard to decide when it's Shakespeare talking and when it's one of his characters, because they are so intimately knit together.

Nevertheless, I feel that by studying his work and what we know of his life, we can learn valuable lessons in leadership that serve us well right to the present day.

Believe you can and you're halfway there.
Theodore Roosevelt

SHAKESPEARE ON COURAGE

Our doubts are traitors,
And make us lose the good we oft might win,
By fearing to attempt.
Measure for Measure

COURAGE, OR HOW TO BE A LEADER IN TIMES OF CRISIS

Cowards die many times before their deaths.
The valiant never taste of death but once.
Julius Caesar

Be there! In times of crisis, it is critical for a leader to have the courage to be present, to face the crisis head-on. A leader needs to be on the spot as soon as possible: assessing the situation, listening to those involved and taking charge. This is the time people most need a leader.

During the course of the American Civil War, President Abraham Lincoln spent most of his time on the move, meeting generals and cabinet ministers, and touring fortifications, battlefields, hospitals and the War Department's Telegraph Office to keep himself up to date with the latest developments. As well as facing a crisis head-on, a leader has to be actively involved at a grassroots level, not just handing down missives from on high.

In World War II, England's King George VI and his queen, Elizabeth, earned the devotion of their subjects by refusing to abandon London and seek a safe haven during the Blitz. They stayed on in Buckingham Palace, making regular forays into bombed areas to comfort the citizens. Their courage was compounded by the presence of Prime Minister Winston Churchill. His stirring oratory and bulldog tenacity radiated hope and resolve not just in Britain but throughout the Free World.

History has few examples of leadership to match that displayed in Britain during World War II.

But you don't have to be in a position of power to be an inspiring leader in tough times. From their various prison cells Mahatma Gandhi, Nelson Mandela and Václav Havel fought against oppressive regimes. Mandela and Havel then went on to become presidents of their respective countries.

***

Let's look further back in history to another legendary leader and see how he found courage in a crisis. Henry V (1386–1422) ruled England from 1413 until his death. In 1415, his excuses for invading France were dubious at best, but we are after all dealing with a medieval monarch whose reputation was based on his prowess in war and his acquisition of territory.

Henry faces his first crisis during the attack on Harfleur in Normandy. His men make a breach in the city walls but then fall back in confusion. In Shakespeare's account, Henry rallies them with a speech notable for its bellicosity as much as its enthusiasm: it's the kind of thing you'd expect from a footy coach at half-time to a team not kicking goals:

> Once more unto the breach, dear friends, once more;
> Or close the wall up with our English dead!
> In peace there's nothing so becomes a man
> As modest stillness and humility:
> But when the blast of war blows in our ears,
> Then imitate the action of the tiger:
> Stiffen the sinews, summon up the blood,
> Disguise fair nature with hard-favoured rage;
> ...
> Now set the teeth and stretch the nostril wide,
> Hold hard the breath, and bend up every spirit
> To his full height! On, on, you noblest English

Whose blood is fet from fathers of war-proof;
Fathers that, like so many Alexanders,
Have in these parts from morn till even fought,
And sheath'd their swords for lack of argument.
Dishonour not your mothers: now attest
That those whom you call'd fathers did beget you.
Be copy now to men of grosser blood,
And teach them how to war. And you, good yeomen,
Whose limbs were made in England, show us here
The mettle of your pasture; let us swear
That you are worth your breeding, which I doubt not,
For there is none of you so mean and base,
That hath not noble lustre in your eyes.
I see you stand like greyhounds in the slips,
Straining upon the start. The game's afoot:
Follow your spirit, and upon this charge
Cry 'God for Harry, England, and Saint George!'

Shakespeare anatomized Henry's tactics; I'll translate the speech a little to make them clearer.

Attack the walls once more, dear friends (it's a nice touch to address the troops as 'dear friends' – very disarming to give them such status), just one more time, or let's die in the attempt.

In peacetime it's fine to be tranquil and civilised, but when the trumpet of war sounds, turn yourself into a wild beast; transform your whole body into a fighting machine. (The speech here escalates into hyperbole that is emotive rather than rational.)

Come on, you *noblest* English (touch of jingoism here); your fathers were men of iron, each as great as Alexander. They once fought in these same French fields from dawn till dusk, then put away their swords because there was no one left to fight.

If you love your mums don't let men call you a pack of bastards – prove that you really are your fathers' sons! (A hint of misogyny there with a dash of emotional blackmail.)

Set an example to these men of inferior race and show them what real fighting is like. (A spicy morsel of contempt and xenophobia.)

And you true-born Englishmen, demonstrate the quality of your homeland and convince me you are worthy of it.

I don't doubt that, because even the lowliest of you looks like a hero. I see that you are itching for a fight; go for it, and let your battle cry be 'For God, King and Country!'

As a born orator Henry can read the moves and knows what buttons to press. If you're asking men to commit mayhem and murder there's no point being subtle about it: a bit of jingoism, a little xenophobia, a mention of home and family along with a dose of blood-lust are what they need to get them over that wall.

The speech may be defined as *leadership in the raw*. It is momentarily effective and could be seen as a template for a motivational speech for any military commander in a do-or-die situation. I can imagine it in the mouth of George Patton, the American Army general known for his colourful speeches in World War II. (One of his famed lines was, 'The object of war is not to die for your country, but to make the other bastard die for his.')

But strip away the speech's finery and it is a brutal, ugly and manipulative piece of oratory.

This is not the mindset you want of a leader in peacetime.

    A far more edifying example of inspirational oratory is found later in Shakespeare's play. After his initial victory at Harfleur, Henry presses on through the French countryside. He meets his setbacks as soldiers fall ill and morale begins to droop. But Henry's presence among his troops is emphasised all the way through the story. He shares their hardships in the mud and rain, and moves among them listening to their fears; comforting, persuading and quenching their doubts. Eventually his depleted and exhausted army is confronted at Agincourt by a French force that outnumbers it five to one.

    Henry knows that this time bombastic rhetoric isn't going to work. He has to find a way of inspiring his followers with language that is simple, plain and homely. He has to persuade them that despite the odds they are about to achieve a glorious victory – that it will be famous until the end of time and they will be envied by all who are not here to share it with them. (Thanks to Shakespeare, this promise has been fulfilled.) Henry plays low status, moves among his men, addresses them by name and calls them his band of brothers. He has nothing to sell them but the notion that 'this day' (the Feast Day of two very obscure saints named Crispin and

Crispian) is a very special one and he hammers home the idea by using 'this day' or 'today' or 'Saint Crispin's Day' more than half-a-dozen times. It works: the name of the day assumes a special kind of glamour and is a lesson in how much spin can be attached to a simple phrase. The speech – easygoing, humorous, confident and persuasive – is undoubtedly one of the great motivational speeches of all time:

> This day is call'd the Feast of *Crispian* .
> He that outlives this day, and comes safe home
> Will stand a tiptoe when this day is nam'd,
> And rouse him at the name of Crispian.
> He that shall live this day, and see old age,
> Will yearly on the vigil feast his neighbours,
> And say 'Tomorrow is Saint Crispian.'
> Then will he strip his sleeve and show his scars.
> And say 'These wounds I had on Crispin's day.'
> Old men forget: yet all shall be forgot,
> But he'll remember with advantages
> What feats he did that day: then shall our names.
> Familiar in his mouth as household words
> Harry the king, Bedford and Exeter,
> Warwick and Talbot, Salisbury and Gloucester,

Be in their flowing cups freshly remember'd.
This story shall the good man teach his son;
And Crispin Crispian shall ne'er go by,
From this day to the ending of the world,
But we in it shall be remember'd;
We few, we happy few, we band of brothers;
For he to-day that sheds his blood with me
Shall be my brother; be he ne'er so vile,
This day shall gentle his condition:
And gentlemen in England now a-bed
Shall think themselves accurs'd they were not here,
And hold their manhoods cheap whiles any speaks
That fought with us upon Saint Crispin's day.

Through brilliant tactics, courage and inspirational oratory, Henry leads his men to a stunning victory. (The oratory, of course, is all Shakespeare's own; we'll never know what the real Henry said that day.)

But you don't have to be a great orator to be a good leader. For me the best examples of Henry's leadership are not his two famous speeches but his general relationship with his troops and understanding what they need from him. Here is Shakespeare's description of Henry's behaviour the night before the decisive Battle of Agincourt:

> The poor condemn'd English,
> Like sacrifices, by their watchful fires,
> Sit patiently and inly ruminate
> The morning's danger; and their gesture sad
> Investing lank-lean cheeks and war-worn coats
> Presenteth them unto the gazing moon
> So many horrid ghosts. O now, who will behold
> The royal captain of this ruin'd band
> Walking from watch to watch, from tent to tent,
> Let him cry 'Praise and glory on his head!'
> For forth he goes and visits all his host.
> Bids them good morrow with a modest smile
> And calls them brothers, friends and countrymen.
> Upon his royal face there is no note
> How dread an army hath enrounded him;
> Nor doth he dedicate one jot of colour
> Unto the weary and all-watch'd night,
> But freshly looks and over-bears attaint

> With cheerful semblance and sweet majesty;
> That every wretch, pining and pale before,
> Beholding him, plucks comfort from his looks:
> A largess universal like the sun
> His liberal eye doth give to every one,
> Thawing cold fear, that mean and gentle all,
> Behold, as may unworthiness define,
> A little touch of Harry in the night.

Here are the hallmarks of good leadership: empathy, modesty, generosity, confidence and optimism. In this situation oratory is uncalled for – actions are enough.

In the vein of Henry V, an important part of my leadership style is leading from the front as well as being part of the team. While being the founder and artistic director of the Nimrod and Bell Shakespeare, I was also directing and acting in most productions. This meant I spent much of my time in the rehearsal room – on the factory floor, you might say – and on stage, and this made for a pretty democratic atmosphere. I was putting myself out there in front of an audience with the rest of the gang, receiving both the kicks and the plaudits alongside them. I also always made time to drop into the scenery workshop and the costume department, and have a cup of tea with the people in marketing, publicity, finance and development, to reaffirm how important every single person is to the success of a production (it's not just the people on stage who make the show). I might have led from the front but I remained part of the team.

Shakespeare's Henry V offers a great snapshot of courage in a time of crisis, of leadership in *action*. What inspiration can we gain from it?

- Get out of your ivory tower and mingle with the troops.
- Whatever your own fears and weariness, you put your troops first.
- You visit them one by one.
- You put on a cheerful face and greet each one as a friend.
- You display no fear or anxiety.
- You show not weariness, but optimism, and your positive energy melts their apprehension.
- Know every member of your team by name and know something about them as individuals.
- Make every one of them feel valued.
- Don't pull rank; instead display humility and lead from the front, but as one of the team, one of 'a band of brothers'.

- Express gratitude to those who have helped you to the top.

***

Another monarch who faces the crisis of the battlefield is Richard III, the antithesis of the kingly virtues exemplified by Henry V.

Whatever the historical reality, Shakespeare's portrait of Richard III is that of a black-hearted villain who plots and murders his way to the crown, eliminating all opposition. But of his physical courage there is no doubt. He has been brought up in the hard school of the Wars of the Roses and from an early age has been party to treachery and butchery.

Sick of his tyranny and cruelty, Richard's nobles desert him one by one and at Bosworth he finds himself facing the forces of his nemesis, the Earl of Richmond. His last card is the army of Lord Stanley, whose son he keeps as a hostage. But finally Stanley deserts him too, willing to risk his son's life to save the crown.

Almost totally deserted, Richard rallies his remaining troops in warlike vein:

> Fight, gentlemen of England! Fight, bold yeomen!
> Draw, archers, draw your arrows to the head!

> Spur your proud horses hard and ride in blood.
>
> ...
>
> A thousand hearts are great within my bosom.
> Advance our standards, set upon our foes;
> Our ancient word of courage, fair Saint George,
> Inspire us with the spleen of fiery dragons!
> Upon them! Victory sits on our helms!

Richard is not just talk; he follows through with desperate prowess:

> CATESBY: The king enacts more wonders than a man,
> Daring an opposite to every danger.
> His horse is slain, and all on foot he fights,
> Seeking for Richmond in the throat of death.
>
> ...
>
> RICHARD: A horse! A horse! My kingdom for a horse!

He might have been a black-hearted villain, but the last of the House of Plantagenet goes down fighting.

A stark contrast to these classic leadership models stands their ancestor Richard II, who also faces a challenge to his crown. But he is too easily deflated – he throws in the towel and abdicates:

> RICHARD: For God's sake let us sit upon the ground
> And tell sad stories of the death of kings
> ...I live with bread like you, feel want,
> Taste grief, need friends; subjected thus,
> How can you say to me I am a king?

Richard II displays a catastrophic failure of leadership, a failure of courage. He still has the crown and the authority to command. But he lacks the guts, the daring and the passion to prevail against all odds that define a leader in a time of crisis.

***

From my own personal experience, I learned that if a crisis is looming the worst thing you can do is hunker down and pretend it's not happening. Better to act quickly and try to head off disaster. In two instances at Bell Shakespeare we called in outside help – skilled facilitators who could take an objective view, offer tough pragmatic advice and be recognised by all parties as an impartial referee with no personal agenda.

One of these crises involved the sudden departure of a general manager. Rather than scramble to find an immediate replacement, we decided on the rather unusual step of running the company by committee, without a general manager. Each department was to become autonomous, but report at weekly meetings to myself and my co-director.

The first step was for the two of us to interview each staff member separately and encourage them to tell us what they thought was wrong with the company, where it was falling short, how it might improve and whether they had any suggestions or ideas for its future course. This was highly discreet and confidential, although we took extensive notes of each conversation. We were impressed by how frank these interviews were, how much people appreciated being consulted and listened to, how many positive ideas were forthcoming, and how little angst there was.

When the interviews were concluded, we collated all the material, called the company together and relayed their ideas and suggestions anonymously. The subsequent boost in morale and cohesiveness was both substantial and long lasting. A new level of trust and mutual respect was established. There was a renewed sense of confidence in a leadership that solicited ideas, listened to them and was prepared to act on them.

Of course, as always, the main issue that emerged was communication, so frequently honoured more in the breach than in the observance – the need for regular, informative company meetings and senior management meetings; the guarantee that no one has misunderstood strategy or has gone off and acted unilaterally; the desire for the left hand to always know what the right hand is up to. Basic stuff, but it's amazing how easily things can fall through the cracks, leaving people aggrieved at not being kept in the loop.

One valuable lesson that we, as leaders, learned from these one-on-one conversations was a reassessment of individual skills, aspirations and temperaments. We decided to overhaul company structure to make the most of individual talents rather than try to squeeze people into existing job descriptions. It taught us to be flexible, to make people more upwardly mobile rather than being siloed.

An immediate result was to make the receptionist a head of department, a role she filled admirably. Making people responsible and semi-autonomous brings out the best in them.

The absence of a general manager also gave us the opportunity for a reality check of our whole operation. We set about minimising our financial losses with an austerity programme for the next two years – smaller venues and shorter seasons meant lower rentals and less expenditure on materials and salaries. Smaller casts and tighter budgets were introduced. A more severe assessment of budget over-runs and risk management was undertaken, alongside a repertoire of sure-fire box office hits – nothing too experimental. A lot of effort was put into social media marketing, with outstanding results. We lowered our box office expectations to a more realistic forecast and, all in all, turned the company's financial situation around to achieve a healthy surplus.

So the experiment was a good one with a very positive outcome. After six months, however, it became clear that we did in fact need a general manager, someone who was always at home base while my co-director and I were in the rehearsal room, in the theatre, or away on tour, as was frequently the case. Our former company manager stepped up into the general manager's job and proved to be an inspired choice. Without the courage to take a different, unexpected leadership approach, we would not have achieved these positive changes at a time of crisis.

A more expected – and still important – leadership approach is to hold team meetings. Regular company meetings have been an important part of Bell Shakespeare's success: an opportunity at least once a month for the whole company to come together and be fully briefed on the company's current position, aspirations and strategies, with detailed reports from all heads of department.

The company meeting always includes some time out for brainstorming and encouraging individuals to float blue-sky ideas, which may find a place at the next planning day with the board and senior management.

These meetings need to be tightly structured with a precise agenda, and yet feel open-ended enough to allow time for debate.

One of the trickiest things is how to physically arrange the room. I find that if you gather people around a long board table, you need at least two rows of chairs. The senior people tend to sit at the table and the more junior ones take to the back row, so you immediately have an undesirable hierarchical and slightly intimidating scenario – and one that doesn't encourage frank and spontaneous discussion.

I've tried taking meetings out of the office and into a big empty rehearsal room with everyone sitting in a circle, so that nobody is at the head of the table and there is a statement of equality. The only problem with this arrangement is that, with a staff of some thirty, the circle is quite large and is intimidating in a different sort of way. You feel as if you're in the spotlight when you speak up and you feel self-conscious in having to project your voice across the space.

I've yet to find the ideal solution, but I'd encourage you to go to some trouble to find a space and a seating configuration that makes people feel at ease and all the more likely to contribute ideas.

Now with so many people working from home and so many meetings via video call, the situation is different, but the challenge is the same: to make sure everyone has a voice and no one is intimidated, afraid of speaking out. That is the challenge for the chair.

Asking each department to deliver a report empowers them and earns them the respect and admiration of the rest of the company, as they outline their tasks, targets and strategies. So often each department is unaware of what others are doing, hence undervalue their contribution.

It's important that the staff have an ongoing relationship with the board of directors and that both sides get to know each other and gain an understanding of each other's roles. Too often staff can see the directors as a bunch of suits who meet in a secret huddle and hand down decisions from on high. When you put faces to the suits and get to know them at social occasions, a much stronger bonding of the company can ensue.

Invariably I find the directors themselves are mightily impressed by hearing reports direct from the coalface, and understanding the myriad concerns and challenges involved in mounting a stage production (or whatever you and your team are undertaking). From out front it always looks so easy, as it should.

Another important feature of company meetings is the opportunity to reiterate the company's message and overall vision. As circumstances change, as people leave and new people join the staff, it's frightening how quickly the mission statement can become blurred or misunderstood. People who leave may take a lot of the company's memory with them, and relationships with various stakeholders (carefully cultivated over many years) can fall by the wayside. You can never take it for granted that everyone is on message. It needs to be constantly restated.

To lead your team, take inspiration from Henry's relationship and communication with his troops: involve them, communicate with them, listen to them, and then have the courage to take action.

***

What can we learn from Shakespeare on courage and leadership?
- Be there! Be visible and be in the thick of it. Take charge.
- Talk to everybody, listen to everybody. Don't be afraid to seek the advice of experts.
- Don't play the blame game or play politics with a crisis. Take responsibility.
- Your actions will speak louder than your words (but if you have the oratorial gifts of a Henry V or a Winston Churchill, use them – inspiration will be welcome).
- Empathise with everybody's hardships and anxieties. Quell their doubts.
- Keep up the praise and encouragement.
- Persevere against the odds. Better to go down fighting than throw in the towel.
- Try to foresee a crisis and have strategies planned.
- Formulate a plan of action as soon as is possible and make it known to all.
- Don't procrastinate. You'll drain your team of energy and optimism.
- You've been given authority. Have the courage to use it.

I learned that courage was not the absence of fear, but the triumph over it.
Nelson Mandela

SHAKESPEARE ON TIMING

There is a tide in the affairs of men,
Which, taken at the flood, leads on to fortune;
Omitted, all the voyage of their life
Is bound in shallows and in miseries.
Julius Caesar

DECISIVENESS, TIMING AND TOUGH DECISIONS

I wasted time and now doth time waste me.
Richard II

Timing, as every stand-up comedian knows, is everything. To gain a deeper understanding of its importance to leadership, it is instructive to study the strategies behind decisive battles from ancient times to the present day – whether it be the tactics of Pericles, Caesar, Napoleon, Rommel and Monash or noted battles such as Marathon, Stalingrad and the Coral Sea.

It's not enough to have your strategies and supplies in place, a favourable terrain and superior numbers. The decision when and where to strike can be the decider. (It's also sobering to note how many famous victories have been the result of good luck rather than good management.)

At the Stratford-on-Avon grammar school the young Shakespeare spent a lot of his time studying the Greek and Roman classics. (He also had to debate in Latin, and argue each side of a topic with equal conviction – great training for a dramatist.) The life and works of Julius Caesar were high on the agenda. So when it came to writing *Julius Caesar,* Shakespeare had to stick pretty closely to what was accepted as historical fact. His audience knew the history as well as he did and would have hissed his taking too many liberties. But as a dramatist he was free to posit the motivations and personalities of his protagonists.

Mark Antony (83–30BC) was a Roman politician whose sense of timing (at least early in his career) was impeccable. He seized the day with a vengeance. When we first meet him in Shakespeare's *Julius Caesar,* he is an indolent playboy with little interest in the political brew stirring around him. When Caesar voices his suspicions of Cassius – 'He thinks too much. Such men are dangerous' – Antony laughs it off:

> Fear him not, Caesar, he's not dangerous;
> He is a noble Roman and well given.

Unaware of the plot to assassinate Caesar, Antony is led aside by one of the conspirators while the others stab Caesar to death. When general panic breaks out Antony flees from the scene, but then sends to the assassins, begging to know the reasons for their action and pledging friendship with all of them. Solemnly he shakes hands with them one by one (carefully taking their names) and asks permission to speak at Caesar's funeral. Cassius warns against this but Brutus overrules him and permits Antony to speak.

This is a fatal mistake. Brutus underestimates Antony's duplicity and brilliance as an orator. Antony quickly turns the crowd against the 'liberators', reminding them of Caesar's glories and contribution to the state, reducing them to tears with a melodramatic account of Caesar's death (which he didn't actually see), appealing to the greed of the crowd by reading from Caesar's will the legacies he has bequeathed them and finally inflaming them to vengeance so that they pursue the assassins out of the city.

When I directed this scene in my production for Bell Shakespeare I had Antony show the audience Caesar's 'will': it was a blank piece of paper. This is justified by Shakespeare himself when, in the scene following the funeral, Antony sends Lepidus to Caesar's house to fetch his actual will so that they can tamper with it. If Antony is only now sending for the will, what was the piece of paper he flourished to the mob earlier?

Shakespeare took his cue from his chief source, Greek philosopher Plutarch, who noted that Antony did a bit of a fiddle with Caesar's will. In the Bell version, I wanted to stress the outrageous showmanship and manipulative nature of Antony's speech – I even had him sign a few autographs and kiss a baby on his way down from the pulpit.

Antony may well have the deep affection for Caesar that he professes; indeed it may be that which spurs him into action. But either way, it's this crisis that enables him to find his voice, flex his power and seize the moment just as Caesar did when he crossed the Rubicon and as Napoleon did by firing 'a whiff of grapeshot' at the rebels of Toulon in 1795, paving his way to becoming Emperor of the French. The timing of their actions calls to mind the old saying, 'Cometh the hour, cometh the man.'

At Philippi the army of Brutus and Cassius faces the army of Anthony and Octavius Caesar, the nephew of Julius, who are seeking to avenge his assassination. The night before the battle they have to make a crucial decision about when and where to attack. Cassius advises delay:

> 'Tis better that the enemy seek us;
> So shall he waste his means, weary his soldiers,
> Doing himself offence, whilst we, lying still,
> Are full of rest, defence and nimbleness.

But Brutus overrules him, pointing out that the local population is hostile and will very likely defect to Antony. He argues that their own army is now at its peak and should strike immediately before it starts to decline:

> On such a full sea are we now afloat,
> And we must take the current when it serves,
> Or lose our ventures.

Although he is the older and more experienced soldier, Cassius defers to Brutus. He has deferred to Brutus a number of times before, with disastrous consequences. Yet now, at this fatal moment, he defers again. Why?

Brutus has a strong and somewhat obstinate personality. He is renowned for his integrity and had taken part in the plot against Caesar solely for the preservation of the Republic. Cassius, on the other hand, is aware that he himself acted partly out of envy and resentment that Caesar had reached such heights, leaving his old companions behind. Moreover he has just now had a furious bust-up with Brutus and been bawled out by him for selling off some army commissions for cash, and protecting fellow officers for doing the same.

Browbeaten and shamefaced by this falling-out, Cassius is too ready to back down and acquiesce in a battle plan he feels in his heart is a mistake. As things turn out, he was right: he and Brutus are overwhelmed by the enemy and forced to commit suicide. The disaster was due to bad timing. Brutus's gut feeling is, 'Now we are at our peak – now is the time to attack.' Cassius's gut tells him, 'No, let's sit tight and let the other fellow wear himself out in seeking us.' On such decisions are battles won or lost.

***

The same crucial question of timing may lead to a government winning or losing an election, a company succeeding in a deal or takeover, and many of the less newsworthy but still important decisions in our daily lives.

My Bell Shakespeare Company faced its first existential crisis at the end of our first season in 1991.

Our mothership, the Australian Elizabethan Trust, went into liquidation and we were cut adrift. All members of our board of directors who were also on the board of the Trust had to resign, leaving just three of us. Without the Trust we were not eligible for tax deductibility, meaning we would have zero chance of attracting sponsors or donations and could not survive. Our new chair, Virginia Henderson, took immediate and decisive action. The next morning she and I flew to Canberra, bailed up the relevant bureaucrats and secured tax deductibility for Bell as a new independent entity. That swift action – that understanding of the importance of timing – saved our bacon.

Some people are *too* impatient when it comes to seizing the day. Take the case of Macbeth. Like Julius Caesar, Macbeth was a real historical figure, but a much more shadowy one. He was born in Scotland around 1005 and ruled the country until his death in 1057. His life story is shrouded in mystery, and Shakespeare uses it as an exercise in ambition, guilt and paranoia.

Macbeth is set up as a man of integrity and valour. He has everything going for him. He has just led successful campaigns against the Scottish rebels and the Norwegian invaders. He is a close favourite of his king and kinsman, the saintly Duncan. And to cap it all, he has just encountered three weird women who seem to have the power of second sight. They prophesy that he will soon be made the Thane of Cawdor and, in time, be crowned King of Scotland.

Left alone, he is perplexed by this prophecy, which touches too closely his secret ambitions. His perplexity is compounded a moment later when messengers from King Duncan arrive with the good news that the king has named him Thane of Cawdor in recognition of his services. Infinite possibilities open in his mind and, tellingly, one of his first instincts urges the murder of King Duncan. He immediately quashes the impulse but writes to his wife to inform her of the uncanny coincidence.

Lady Macbeth has none of her husband's qualms. On reading his letter, her immediate decision is that she and her husband must dispatch Duncan and seize the crown. This resolution receives approbation when news arrives that Duncan is on his way to spend the night under the roof of the Macbeths at Inverness. It seems to her that it is meant to be.

Macbeth rushes in, full of excitement, and she stops him in his tracks with the proposition that they kill Duncan that very night. Macbeth tries to postpone a decision, but not for long. At dinner he absents himself from the table, his mind in a turmoil, but his wife's steely resolve convinces him to proceed with the murder and they cook up a hasty plan to get the king's bodyguards drunk and pin the killing on them and the king's sons, Malcolm and Donalbain.

What's the rush behind this crazy, ill-hatched plan? The weird sisters' prophecy about the Thane of Cawdor came true, so why should not the promise of the crown as well? All Macbeth has to do is wait. Why commit the most heinous crime of regicide – the victim being, what's more, your friend, mentor and kinsman? And if you're going to do it, is there not a smarter choice than under your own roof? A more neutral, less suspicious time and place? A better strategy and cover-up?

The chief motivation is, of course, unbridled ambition coupled with impatience and recklessness. A bit of background might throw some light on this. They are living in a time of war, rebellion and uncertainty. There is no established plan of succession. Any one of the powerful thanes could make a bid for the crown; but Macbeth has some reason to expect, after his recent stunning victories, that he will be chosen by his fellows to succeed Duncan. The king throws a spanner in the works by naming his eldest son, Malcolm, as his successor, and from a leader as revered as Duncan this carries a lot of weight.

And Macbeth is not the only contender. His fellow general Banquo has also scored great success and has been told by the weird sisters that, although he will not be king himself, he will be the father to a long line of kings: a dynasty!

In other words, Macbeth is justified in seeing himself surrounded by rivals and, if he doesn't act quickly, opportunity may pass him by. Nevertheless, the assassination and its aftermath are very poorly planned and nobody believes the

Macbeths' story for long. So, on timing, Shakespeare makes the following clear:
- By all means seize the day boldly, but only when you've done the sums and figured the consequences.
- Beware of impatience. It can lead you into folly. Not everything comes to one who waits, but just a little breathing space might lead you to making a wiser decision.
- Think first not of what you stand to gain but what you have to lose.
- Your gut feeling may be compelling, but check it against the gut feelings of your colleagues; maybe you are mistaking rashness and bravado for inspiration.

***

The opposite of decisiveness and seizing the day is procrastination and the fear of making tough decisions. This can afflict either leaders themselves or the people they lead.

During the American Civil War, Abraham Lincoln was driven almost to distraction by the procrastination of many of his generals, who seemed overwhelmed by the task they faced: one after another, Winfield Scott, Irvin McDowell, George B. McClellan, Henry Halleck, John McClernand, Nathaniel Banks and William

Rosecrans all let him down by their inertia and indecision.

At times Lincoln had to take command himself. In May 1862 he travelled to Fort Monroe to initiate action and ordered the assault on Norfolk, Virginia. It was only when Lincoln appointed Ulysses S. Grant as lieutenant-general in 1864 that things started to move.

A leader must not be afraid of squashing a few toes and taking over when subordinates are not pulling their weight.

Leadership can entail making some tough decisions. In nearly fifty years of running theatre companies I have fired only three people. It was an unpleasant thing to do. I am fully aware of the damage to a person's reputation, work prospects and peace of mind if they are sacked. But in each of these cases I felt totally justified. Their ongoing presence threatened the stability of the enterprise. There was too much at risk, too many other people to consider.

Henry V dispenses with a few people along the way, but he does it more coolly than I could manage. First there's Jack Falstaff, the feisty and riotous drinking companion of Henry's youth. Falstaff is great fun to have around. His wit, energy and lust for life are incomparable. But he is also totally disreputable: a thief, drunkard and outrageous liar. Henry warns him that once he becomes king, Falstaff will no longer be welcome in his circle of friends. But Falstaff refuses to heed the warning and is heartbroken when he is dumped after Henry's coronation.

On the evening of setting sail with his army bound for France, Henry is tipped off that three of his knights, Cambridge, Scroop and Grey, have accepted money from France to assassinate him. Surrounded by his lords, Henry faces the three and accuses them of treason:

> You have conspired against our royal person,
> Joined with an enemy proclaimed, and from his coffers
> Received the golden earnest of our death;
> Wherein you would have sold your king to slaughter
> ...
> And his whole kingdom into desolation.
> Touching our person seek we no revenge;
> But we our kingdom's safety must so tender,
> Whose ruin you have sought, that to her laws
> We do deliver you. Get you therefore hence,
> Poor miserable wretches, to your death...

Adamant though he is, Henry is clearly distressed by this treachery, especially in the case of Lord Scroop, a close friend:

> But oh,
> What shall I say to thee, Lord Scroop,
> thou cruel,
> Ingrateful, savage and inhuman creature?
> Thou that didst bear the key of all my counsels,
> That knew'st the very bottom of my soul
> ...
> I will weep for thee;
> For this revolt of thine, methinks, is like
> Another fall of man.

Despite this display of affection, Henry wastes no time in sending all three traitors to the block.

Friendship with Henry is no guarantee of safety. During the march towards Agincourt a soldier is brought before the king, accused of robbing a church. The soldier is his old friend Bardolph, one of Falstaff's drinking buddies.

There is a historical record of this incident but the soldier in question is anonymous. Shakespeare goes to the pains of making him familiar to us to make Henry's decision all the harder. But Henry shows no hesitation —

Bardolph must be made an example of and is hanged:

> HENRY: We would have all offenders so cut off: and we give express charge that in our marches through the country there be nothing compelled from the villages, nothing taken but paid for, none of the French upbraided or abused in disdainful language; for when lenity and cruelty play for a kingdom, the gentler gamester is the soonest winner.

Discipline and strategy trump old friendships.

Henry was called on to make another tough decision during the Battle of Agincourt. When repeated French cavalry charges failed, bogged down in the muddy battlefield, thousands of French knights surrendered and offered themselves for ransom. They were herded together with other prisoners and held under guard. Henry's victory was looking assured, but he was suddenly warned that a French counterattack was about to take place. He immediately ordered the slaughter of all prisoners to prevent them rallying against him. Even by medieval standards, this was a savage order. The English soldiers were dismayed: they were counting on rich rewards from the prisoners' ransoms.

Arguments have raged among historians ever since as to the justification of Henry's action: some denouncing it as a war crime, others defending it as a regrettable but expedient tactic. Shakespeare is ambivalent, but leaves us with the reaction of Captain Fluellen, an ardent admirer of the king. He compares Henry to Alexander the Great, reminding us that Alexander killed his best friend Clitus, just as Henry broke the heart of Jack Falstaff, and adds:

> The king most worthily hath caused every soldier to cut his prisoner's throat. O! 'tis a gallant king.

A fervent admirer will see only a positive side to whatever their hero says or does. The irony cannot be missed.

***

When directing a stage production I find myself having to make decisions, to be decisive every hour of the day.

Decisiveness, however, does not mean bullying. A really good theatre production depends on an integration of the entire company, on strong and supportive relationships that add a tangible extra layer to what happens onstage — a culture of sharing, passing the ball and looking after each other.

Good examples can be found in the circus, where trapeze artists depend entirely on their mate being there to catch them and thus develop, over time, the subtlest awareness of rhythm, energy and timing.

So how do I develop a cast of actors where some are inevitably older, more experienced and playing larger roles than the young newcomers?

First I ask the small-part players what extra skills they have. If someone replies 'juggling' or 'tap-dancing', I say, 'Great, let's start each rehearsal with twenty minutes of juggling and tap-dancing.' It's a great warm-up, it breaks down barriers, no one minds looking silly and it empowers the small-part players, giving them a bit of status and earning the respect of the rest of the cast. Others might lead us in voice exercises, or some form of physical warm-up.

When it comes to giving notes or feedback at the end of a rehearsal, I have the cast sit in a circle so that they're all of equal status. After I've given my notes, I throw the session open to general discussion – any ideas? Any suggestions? Do you feel we're on the right track? I canvass all opinions and don't dismiss any out of hand.

Having heard everyone, I'll say, 'Thank you all for your ideas. They are all interesting, but I'm going to choose this one to go with.' Since everyone has had a chance to be heard and taken seriously, there is no resentment about the decision, and the cast feel bound in a common cause.

Decisiveness also plays an essential part in securing a leader's legacy. Leaving a company or business you have built or have led is a significant decision to make. When I decided it was time to leave Bell Shakespeare, I took a strategic approach. I had seen one or two other companies flounder when the artistic director or CEO departed suddenly, so I planned a long and smooth transition. I chose my successor and invited him to become first my associate director and then my co-artistic director, and over the course of the next two years I stepped back little by little, ceding more responsibility to him.

When I formally stepped down at the end of 2015, it was a smooth, seamless transition. I resisted any suggestion that I might stay on the board or have any formal ongoing role with the company, because I think a clean break is essential and I wanted to give my successor a clear run, not stay hovering around and looking over his shoulder. A tough decision, but the right one.

***

What does Shakespeare teach us about timing and decisiveness?
- Beware the leader who promises a quick fix. For every complex problem there is an answer that is quick, simple – and wrong.
- Think fast but think straight; avoid emotional responses and knee-jerk reactions.
- If subordinates fail to live up to expectations, step in and take over.
- Be ready to climb down and reverse decisions.
- Remember that your organisation will take on the personality of its leader.
- Delegate responsibilities – who are your best supporters?
- You may have to make tough decisions. Try to balance pragmatism with compassion. You are dealing with other human beings, not just numbers.

Ninety per cent of leadership is the ability to communicate something people want.

Dianne Feinstein, US senator

SHAKESPEARE ON ABUSE OF POWER

Oh! it is excellent
To have a giant's strength, but it is tyrannous
To use it like a giant
....
...but man, proud man,
Drest in a little brief authority
....
Plays such fantastic tricks before high heaven
As make the angels weep.
Measure for Measure

ARROGANCE

You can disagree without being disagreeable.
Ruth Bader Ginsburg

When a Roman general scored a particularly glorious victory he was accorded a Triumph – meaning he could wear a laurel wreath and ride in a chariot at the head of his troops through the streets of Rome.

The procession was followed by gladiator and wild beast shows in the arena in his honour. But as he rode in triumph in his chariot, a slave stood behind him whispering in his ear, 'Remember you are mortal.' Was this a senatorial device to foster personal humility? Partly. But more importantly, it was to discourage any overweening military ambition. The Senate decreed that any general entering Rome had to leave his troops outside the city limits. A victorious general with a couple of thousand soldiers behind him could potentially stage a military coup. So to ride in triumph through the streets with your troops was an exceptional and jealously guarded privilege.

The Tarquin dynasty of kings had been turfed out of Rome in 509BC by Lucius Junius Brutus, the ancestor of Shakespeare's regicide. The

Roman Republic was determined to quash any return to the monarchy or a military dictatorship, which would be just as bad.

In 49BC, Julius Caesar famously broke this pact, when, returning from his conquest of Gaul, he halted his troops on the banks of the Rubicon, the demarcation line of the city limits. Confident of his reputation and popularity, he made the fateful decision to cross the Rubicon and lead his army into Rome, with the words, 'Let the die be cast!'

This bold act precipitated a civil war, which was resolved in Caesar's favour, resulting in him being appointed dictator for life, and paving the way for his ultimate ambition – to be crowned king.

***

Julius Caesar is Shakespeare's most insightful essay on political rivalry and jockeying for position. The image of being 'stabbed in the back' has become part of our daily discourse, be it political, corporate or simply social.

There are no heroes or villains in this play – our sympathies shift this way and that as we hear various characters' points of view. The play is an essay on how events are shaped by individuals with various strengths and weaknesses; how language can be manipulated to change the course of history; and how cool patience and long-term strategy will win over rashness, impulsiveness and self-deceit. The play is packed with strong personalities and we can learn a lot about leadership, morality and ethics from studying them.

During the Renaissance, Julius Caesar was considered to be one of the Nine Worthies (that is, one of the nine heroes of the ancient world). But he gets a bit of a bum rap from Shakespeare.

According to Roman historians Caesar was a brilliant military strategist who waged successful campaigns in France, Spain, Germany and Britain. He was an accomplished literary stylist and an effective orator. He seems to have been extremely popular with his troops and had 'the common touch' in relation to them. In his writing, Plutarch commented on the difference between Caesar and his great rival, Pompey, preparing their men for battle. Pompey would assemble his troops, then stand before them on a dais and deliver a carefully prepared motivational speech, which the men would applaud at appropriate intervals.

Caesar's approach, however, was far more casual: he would walk around the camp, greeting soldiers and gathering them about him as he strolled. When he had gathered a sufficient number, he'd sit on the back of a vegetable cart and tell filthy jokes. According to one soldier, 'The things that man could do with a carrot would make a donkey laugh.'

Having got the men warmed up and fully on side, Caesar would give the command and lead them into battle. He was also ambitious to a remarkable degree and could be as ruthless a politician as he was a soldier.

At the time of his assassination Caesar was only fifty-two years old, hale and hearty except for a predisposition to epilepsy, which sometimes afflicted him in public.

But Shakespeare plays up Caesar's physical and personality defects; in fact he suggests that Caesar is on the verge of senility. He is going deaf and lacks physical stamina. Shakespeare has the envious Cassius recount an occasion when Caesar challenged him to a swimming race across the Tiber; halfway across Caesar began to drown and had to call on Cassius to rescue him. When he was campaigning in Spain, Cassius recalls, Caesar was taken with a fever and called out for drink like 'a sick girl'. Cassius cannot contain his contempt and resentment:

> ...And this man
> Is now become a god; and Cassius is
> A wretched creature and must bend his body
> If Caesar carelessly but nod on him.

As well as this physical deterioration Shakespeare suggests that a mark of Caesar's decline is an increasingly superstitious frame of mind.

Caesar's wife, Calpurnia, has nightmares forecasting his death and persuades Caesar not to attend a scheduled meeting of the Senate. But the crafty conspirator Decius manages to convince Caesar that all Calpurnia's fears are groundless and that the Senate intends to bestow a crown on him.

This is enough for Caesar to undertake his fatal journey to the Capitol. He doesn't pause to ask, 'What's the catch?' His arrogance wins out.

Why is Shakespeare at such pains to emphasise the weaknesses of a hero so universally admired? It's because he's determined to dig under the surface of popular myth, the PR spin and media bullshit that so often veils public figures from close scrutiny. It's dangerous to eulogise our leaders and turn a blind eye to their foibles: we'll only be disappointed when we see their feet of clay. If we're talking leadership, let's get real; we're talking about real people, not personae constructed by the spin doctors.

At the start of Shakespeare's play we meet Caesar at the height of his power. He has subjugated vast territories for the Republic and is dictator for life – a king in all but name. Yet he still hankers after imperial honours and official godhead status. He is returning in procession from the annual Feast of Lupercal, commemorating the founding of Rome, and things have not gone well.

In a piece of carefully rehearsed stage management, his protégé Mark Antony publicly offers Caesar a crown and three times Caesar wafts it away with his hand to show his disdain for such an honour (although, as Casca observes in the play, 'he was very loath to lay his fingers off it').

The crowd cheers Caesar's display of humility, but then, to spoil it all, 'He fell down in the marketplace and foamed at the mouth, and was speechless.' This epileptic display is not how Caesar wants the mob to remember him.

The embittered Cassius instigates a conspiracy against Caesar. Once they were fellow soldiers. Now Caesar has put himself on a pedestal. He already has the wide-ranging powers of dictator – kingship would make him invulnerable and unstoppable. There is only one remedy: his death.

Cassius sets about recruiting like-minded Republicans to his cause – all of them apprehensive about Caesar's ravenous ambition and totalitarian control.

The hardest one to convince is Marcus Brutus, but he is the frontman Cassius desperately needs. Cassius is under no illusion about the reverence and esteem in which Caesar is held by the general populace, who could very easily lynch the conspirators.

Brutus comes from a noble family and is renowned as a politician of unimpeachable integrity who will be able to sell Caesar's assassination to the mob as a regrettable but necessary action.

Brutus is a bosom-friend of Caesar, but such is his sense of righteousness that he allows himself to be persuaded of the validity of the conspiracy.

On the day of the murder Caesar is lured to the Capitol, despite the warnings of his wife and the soothsayer who admonishes him to 'Beware the ides of March'. He is stabbed to death by the conspirators while the rest of the senators panic and duck for cover. Caesar meets his end bravely, refusing to fall as his enemies stab him, looking Brutus in the eye as his once-friend delivers the death blow. 'Et tu, Brute?' Caesar tragically enquires, continuing with 'Then fall, Caesar,' before collapsing at the base of the statue of Pompey – the enemy he vanquished in the civil war all those years ago.

In theatrical terms, Julius Caesar is a somewhat ambivalent tragic hero. He is often sold short in performance, coming across as a bit of a dotard, a pompous egoist or a figure of fun. To portray him thus diminishes Shakespeare's intention and the series of moral dilemmas the play poses.

Shakespeare's Caesar, as well as being vain, arrogant and overreaching, has sterling qualities. He can be trusting and generous. Before setting out to the Capitol, he invites the conspirators to take a glass of wine, putting his arm around the shoulders of the men who are about to murder him. His self-confidence can make him naïve. But most of the time he is a shrewd judge of character. Noticing Cassius watching from the sidelines, he confides to Mark Antony:

Let me have men about me that are fat;
...
Yond Cassius has a lean and hungry look;
He thinks too much. Such men are dangerous
...
...He reads much.
Such men as he are never at heart's ease
Whiles they behold a greater than themselves,
And therefore are they very dangerous.

He suddenly realises he has said too much, betraying anxiety. So he covers it with a dash of arrogant bravado:
> I rather tell thee what is to be feared
> Than what I fear; for always I am Caesar.

But then another little touch of human weakness as he seeks Mark Antony's opinion:
> Come on my right hand, for this ear is deaf,
> And tell me truly what thou thinkst of him.

However great his past achievements, political shrewdness and largesse of spirit, Caesar is undone by his giant ego, blind ambition and the arrogance that often attends high office. When Decius asks him for some cause why he will not attend the Senate meeting, Caesar loftily replies:
> The cause is in my will: I will not come.
> That is enough to satisfy the Senate.

In the fatal Senate meeting Caesar displays one final flash of arrogance. The senators beseech him to rescind the banishment of one of their fellows. They kneel to him and pray for his mercy. In reply, Caesar dismisses their request, comparing himself to the pole star, the northern star, which alone is fixed and unmoveable:
> I could be well moved if I were as you;

> If I could pray to move, prayers would move me;
> But I am constant as the northern star,
> Of whose true fixed and resting quality
> There is no fellow in the firmament.
> The skies are painted with unnumbered sparks,
> They are all fire, and every one doth shine;
> But there's but one in all doth hold his place.
> So in the world: 'tis furnish'd well with men,
> And men are flesh and blood, and apprehensive;
> Yet in the number I do know but one
> That unassailable holds on his rank,
> Unshaked of motion: and that I am he,
> Let me a little show it...

With that statement Caesar seals his death warrant.

So what can we learn from Shakespeare's portrayal of Caesar?

- Don't rest on your laurels. You can't expect the next generation, who weren't on the long march with you, to hold your past glories of much account, no matter how often you broadcast them.

- Listen to advice: Calpurnia, Caesar's wife, has strong and impeccable intuition, which Caesar underestimated. The soothsayer who warns Caesar to 'Beware the ides of March' equates to the social media, political commentators and press gallery who are pretty aware of what's going on. Ignore them at your peril.
- Keep polishing your skills as a judge of character: look for warning signs, read between the lines, don't take people at face value. Be alert to their personal agendas, especially if they are flattering you. Resist becoming cynical or paranoid, but learn to read the psychological needs and motives of others.
- Remain aware of the political and social environment you are moving in. It's changing all the time. Are you moving with it, or do you risk being left behind, unable to read the signs? Have you a tin ear?
- Learn to appreciate when enough is enough. How much more money, power, property, adulation do you need? Learn to let go and relish contentment.

***

Arrogance and ego – found in most human arenas – can be particularly evident in theatre.

When it comes to directing a show, or any major project, your leadership style boils down to the question: are you a dictator or a collaborator? I've worked with both, I've been both, and I now know which I prefer. You can apply the following observations to most occupations.

Young directors tend towards the dictatorial end of the scale. Partly it's an ego trip but it's also a sign of insecurity, fear that you will be usurped, your authority undermined. It's a signal that you need to be seen as top dog, that you're anxious you'll be 'found out' if you're challenged and that you're worried your 'vision' will be distorted or compromised by others. You feel that being the director your job is to direct, to be solely responsible for the outcome. 'This is my show,' you say.

As you get a little older and more experienced, with a few successes behind you, you can learn to let go of these anxieties and will find that, by throwing open the exercise to full-on collaboration, a much better 'vision' may take shape, a much richer experience shared by all. To have twenty creative people pooling their ideas can be far more stimulating and inventive than you trying to go it alone.

Similarly, when directing actors, one should remember your job isn't to impose a performance on them, but to *elicit* one, and make them feel that they have discovered it for themselves. If the actor has ownership of the performance and is proud of having created it, it will be far easier to sustain night after night than one that has been imposed. This applies to anyone in a managerial position.

Coaxing a performance from an actor rather than dictating it shouldn't be seen as being too soft. The director still has to be rigorous, ask the hard questions and keep raising the stakes, demanding deeper engagement and dismissing half-hearted or lazy responses, the easy options.

In the end, most actors like being pushed beyond what they thought were their limits, knocked out of their comfort zone, made to go further and dig deeper – because, though it may be uncomfortable at the time, they know in their hearts that this is how great performances are made.

The director has to be careful that this sort of rigorous coaching doesn't become an ego trip, transforming the director into a Svengali or Frankenstein figure: 'You are my creature – I made you!'

A bad director – or leader – will take recourse in developing favourites within the cast, or choosing a whipping boy on whom to vent their insecurity. They will create discord and tension in the rehearsal room under the misapprehension that they are creating 'drama'.

They will over-direct, not knowing when to stop and let the actors have their heads. Micromanaging – in any arena – destroys initiative.

A bad director will wreck actors' confidence. A good director, or leader, will always offer positive, constructive criticism and give praise wherever possible. (As the director, my job is to be critical, but it's vital that all criticism is positive and encouraging – never destructive, personal or spiteful.)

A poor director will panic and try to lock down solutions rather than staying open to change up until the last minute. They will lose their temper, cry out for help, show how exhausted they are – all playing for sympathy. (But your actors will secretly despise you; they want you to stay buoyant – you're the leader, after all.)

A bad director will take themself too seriously. Any endeavour has to be fun and approached with a degree of playfulness and light-heartedness. That will help sustain energy and commitment.

Putting on a show is a risky business. So the rehearsal room has to be a safe and encouraging environment where risks can be taken. Arrogance has no place here.

We respect a director – we respect a leader – who is:
- convincing in their ethical behaviour, compassion and generosity
- open to hearing all sides and willing to solicit opinions
- a firm decision-maker not afraid of tough choices
- a keen judge of character
- energetic, respectful, punctual and passionate about the job
- innovative, adventurous, not stuck in the past
- able to think ahead, foresee consequences and make plans
- good-humoured, not 'special', but a first among equals, and
- able to spread a contagious optimism.

***

As we have seen, Caesar embodies many of the best and worst characteristics of leadership. Yet, although the play is called *Julius Caesar*, Caesar's presence in the play is secondary: he is gone halfway through. Brutus, Cassius and Mark Antony get a lot more stage time. Shakespeare is not interested in writing a historical biography;

what interests him is the lead-up to the assassination and its aftermath – how strong personalities and personal agendas shape the course of history.

The other protagonists in the play are more complex than Caesar and probably more interesting. We can revisit Brutus here. Brutus is traditionally regarded as the leading character: a man of great sincerity and integrity, but prone to making disastrous errors of judgement, as we saw earlier. This can be sheeted home, largely, to his own brand of arrogance.

Brutus takes himself a mite too seriously and is a little too impressed with his reputation for probity. This encourages in him a degree of contempt and intolerance for weakness in others, and therefore a readiness to overrule their suggestions without due consideration.

Having been convinced by Cassius that Caesar is a potential tyrant and menace to the Republic, Brutus agonises over the decision to assassinate the man who is his friend, his mentor and the legitimate head of state. Reconciled to the idea that 'it must be by his death', Brutus, however, rejects the suggestion that Caesar should not die alone. Cassius in particular urges that Mark Antony should die with Caesar because he is 'a shrewd contriver' who will turn public opinion against the assassins and take revenge.

But Brutus shrugs off the warning, dismissing Antony as a lightweight 'given to sports, to wildness and much company'.

Regretfully the other conspirators back down. As you may remember from the earlier discussion, after Caesar's death Antony weeps over his corpse and asks permission to speak at his funeral. Cassius is outraged by the idea:

> Brutus, a word with you.
> You know not what you do. Do not consent
> That Antony speak in his funeral.
> Know you how much the people may be moved
> By that which he will utter?

Again, Brutus brushes him aside:
> I will myself into the pulpit first,
> And show the reason of our Caesar's death.

As we know, he totally underestimates Antony's oratorical genius, presuming his own to be superior. But within ten minutes of Antony's taking the stage he has whipped the crowd into a fury with a speech that is a masterpiece of spin, emotional blackmail and downright fabrication. The conspirators flee for their lives but Antony comes after them with an army co-led by Octavius Caesar.

In dismissing Cassius's battle plan to take on the army (recall that Cassius is the older and more experienced soldier), Brutus once more displays his impatience with opinions other than his own. His sense of superiority, of always being right, allows no space for debate.

Adding to the tension was that earlier falling out between the two of them because Cassius was selling off army commissions in exchange for money, and holding back funds that Brutus needed to pay his troops.

Hysterical with fury, Cassius threatens Brutus with physical violence but Brutus wafts him aside with an air of moral superiority bordering on priggishness:

> There is no terror, Cassius, in your threats;
> For I am arm'd so strong in honesty
> That they pass by me as the idle wind
> Which I respect not.

Arrogance can take many forms. From Brutus and Cassius we can learn:
- Have respect for the experience of older wiser heads. They may just be right.
- In an argument, don't dash to your corner and cling to it, deaf to the other person.

- Listen patiently to what the other has to say; weigh it carefully.
- Don't let ego get in the way of making the right decision.
- Don't underestimate your rivals. Observe them carefully and listen to others' opinions of them – you may have missed something.
- Be open to new ideas, new ways of doing things.
- Don't let envy or anger drive your actions the way Cassius did. They will erase your vision of the big picture and make you impulsive and impatient.
- Envy and anger will also tempt you to a course of action lacking in ethics and decency, and thereby destroy your self-respect.
- Even if you feel morally or intellectually superior, have patience with those not so blessed. Seek out your own shortcomings and own up to them. This may make you a little more tolerant of others.
- If, based on all evidence, you're convinced you're right, don't be bullied out of your opinion. Stick to your guns.
- Be magnanimous in victory.

The more informed you are, the less arrogant and aggressive you are.
Nelson Mandela

SHAKESPEARE ON CORRUPTION

Therefore it is meet
That noble minds keep ever with their likes;
For who so firm that cannot be seduced?
Julius Caesar

ENTITLEMENT

And now let's go hand in hand, not one before another.
The Comedy of Errors

A close bedfellow of arrogance is entitlement, that belief that one deserves more, is worthy of more, than others. A sense of entitlement is by no means a rarity in the world we inhabit today. Even in an open and free democracy a lot of people agree with George Orwell's pigs: 'All animals are equal, but some animals are more equal than others.' Entitlement has been lovingly nurtured by the English public school system (and its offshoots in Australia), which for the last three hundred years has produced generations of young men convinced they were born to rule because of their innate superiority to the toiling masses and 'colonials'. Wealth, privilege and power were siphoned off for the favoured few.

Happily we are witnessing the gradual disintegration of this archaic social fabric, but we can only wonder at the tenacity of the gilded darlings clinging to the wreckage.

In the case of Brutus, his arrogance may stem partly from pride in his lineage as a descendent of Lucius Junius Brutus. A family name can hang heavily and weigh one down with clout as well as expectations.

Caesar's parental origins were not particularly noteworthy. He was a self-made man whose arrogance was fanned by his remarkable military feats and the adulation that accompanies them, sustained by a keen intelligence and a talent for politics. Any sense of entitlement felt well earned.

Not so Richard II. Here is a man who believes he can have or do whatever he wants simply because he was born into the purple. Richard is of that medieval mindset that believes in the divine right of kings: that they are God's representatives on Earth and have been put here by Him to rule in His name. Despite King John's concessions in the Magna Carta of 1215, this notion of a monarch's 'divine right' persisted in England until 1649, when Oliver Cromwell beheaded Charles I and declared England to be a Commonwealth. The monarchy was restored in 1660, but the concept of divine right was not resurrected with it.

In the case of Richard II, he surrounds himself with toadies and sycophants who want to bask in his golden glow and keep nasty everyday realities at bay. Unable to decide the right course of justice in a quarrel between two powerful nobles, his cousin Henry Bolingbroke and Sir Thomas Mowbray, Richard decides it would be more expedient to get both of them out of his hair. So he banishes them both, Mowbray for life and Bolingbroke for ten years. With Bolingbroke out of the way, Richard decides it would be very convenient to seize all his land and property and flog it off to pay the costs of his wars in Ireland.

This rash and wanton act infuriates Bolingbroke's friends and followers, so Bolingbroke has no trouble raising an army to topple Richard and take his crown. Fatuously, Richard cannot bring himself to terms with this new reality. Bolingbroke is a pragmatist, a modern man and product of Renaissance scepticism, but Richard is still living in a medieval wonderland, counting on God and His angels to rush to his defence:

> Not all the water in the rough rude sea
> Can wash the balm off from an anointed king;
> The breath of worldly men cannot depose
> The deputy elected by the Lord.
> For every man that Bolingbroke hath pressed
> To lift shrewd steel against our golden crown,
> God for his Richard hath in heavenly pay
> A glorious angel. Then, if angels fight,

> Weak men must fall; for heaven still guards the right.

Richard's faith in a divine rescue party is unfulfilled: he is deposed, imprisoned and shortly after murdered by an ambitious courtier hoping to find favour with Bolingbroke, now Henry IV.

Shakespeare was flirting with danger in putting this story on stage.

Queen Elizabeth I was much vexed by the plotting of her cousin Mary Queen of Scots, who was hoping to depose her. Shakespeare's play cut a bit too close to the bone. After seeing the play, the queen reputedly demanded of her courtiers, 'I am Richard II, know ye not that?' Scenes from the play were banned and Shakespeare and his fellow actors were in deep trouble — fast-talking by friends at court saved their necks.

But this is not the only time Shakespeare questions the special status accorded to a monarch. Consider this remarkable speech:

> I think the king is but a man as I am; the violet smells to him as it doth to me ... and his senses have but human conditions; his ceremonies laid by, in his nakedness he appears but a man...

That speech could be considered seditious, except that Shakespeare puts it in the mouth of a king himself: Henry V, no less – the poster boy for the monarchy. But Henry is much more of a realist than his predecessor Richard II; he is a man who stays in touch with his power base, cultivates 'the common touch' and eschews any hint of entitlement (except when it suits him).

Studying Richard II's delusions of divine right and the resulting entitlement and arrogance, we can learn the following:
- Don't be misled by flatterers bolstering your status and privileges.
- Beware of rashness and impulsiveness. Don't make rash decisions – sleep on them.
- Know how to say *sorry* and admit errors.
- Be aware of the social norms operating around you – come down from your ivory tower and look around.
- Be alert to the private agendas of those you're dealing with.
- Don't force your adversary into a corner – leave room to negotiate.
- Keep a cool head – don't be inflamed by the passions of cronies who may have their own agendas.

***

Sometimes a sense of entitlement is embedded in class snobbery. This is certainly the case of Caius Marcius Coriolanus, one of the most difficult to warm to of all Shakespeare's protagonists. In *Coriolanus* Shakespeare pits the patricians (the ruling class) of ancient Rome against the restive, resentful plebeian class, who are stirred to mutiny by a pair of conniving tribunes (better understood as shop stewards).

Caius Marcius is a fearsome and fearless warrior who leads his ragtag plebeian soldiers in an attack on the enemy town of Corioli. When they fall back, he rushes through the gates and takes the town singlehanded. For this formidable victory he is honoured with the title of 'Coriolanus'.

But his prowess as a fighter is not matched by a talent for diplomacy in peacetime. He makes his contempt for the common people all too obvious and, far from charming them into voting him into high office, he suggests they should be stripped of all rights and privileges and subject themselves to the 'gentry, title and wisdom' of the ruling class.

Like Richard II, Coriolanus is stuck in a time warp where birth and class trump democracy. He cannot see a new order emerging; or if he does, he tries to stamp it out.

Tradition requires that to be elected consul, Coriolanus must stand in the marketplace dressed in a gown of humility and beg the people for their votes. Forced into acting this charade by his forceful and ambitious mother, Coriolanus makes a total botch of it and ends up abusing and alienating the voters.

This suicidal act of hubris is the result of his arrogance born of a sense of entitlement and innate class superiority.

We can profit from his mistakes:
- Learn how to accommodate political realities; you can't stand aloof from them.
- Play along with norms and traditions or you'll offend people by displaying your contempt. Count the number of photographs you've seen of Australian prime ministers putting on unusual hats or traditional costumes overseas (while no doubt privately cursing the camera).
- Reinvent yourself according to the circumstances. Eisenhower managed it, Patton couldn't.

***

When it comes to the arrogance born of entitlement, no story of Shakespeare's has more to say to us than *King Lear,* the ultimate critique of privilege and patriarchy.

Lear bathes in an aura of kingship shot through with even more mystique than that of the Christian kings. Shakespeare sets his tale in pre-Christian Britain, a world of druids and pagan superstition. Lear's status is semi-divine, the lightning rod between the gods and earthly men.

Moreover, he has occupied this exalted position for over seventy years, surrounded by faithful servants and no one to challenge his authority or even his slightest whim. But things are about to change. He is looking forward to abdicating some of his status but hanging on to the perks of office. He anticipates a jolly retirement, making leisurely tours of his territories and staying with each of his three daughters in turn, accompanied by his devoted fool and a hundred roistering knights, his personal bodyguard.

But he is also planning what turns out to be a disastrous succession plan. He will divide his kingdom into three and give a slice to each of his daughters, with the best bit going to the one who publicly professes the greatest love for him. (Secretly he has already earmarked the choicest slice for his favourite, youngest daughter Cordelia.)

This public display of narcissism is both rash and ingenuous. Of course the two older daughters lie their heads off, vying for the best bit of real estate. But Cordelia, the embodiment of innocent integrity, refuses to play the game. Insulted and enraged, Lear disowns her and splits the kingdom between the older sisters, Goneril and Regan, who immediately start plotting how to get rid of him and his noisome rabble of followers. His retinue of a hundred retainers is reduced to fifty, then to twenty-five, then: 'What need you five-and-twenty, ten, or five ... What need one?'

Driven to a despairing rage by this obliteration of his royal status, Lear dashes into the wilderness, where it takes the fury of a violent storm to shake him into an understanding of himself and his place in the cosmos:

> When the rain came to wet me once,
> and the wind to make me chatter, when
> the thunder would not peace at my bidding,
> there I found 'em, there I smelt 'em out.
> Go to, they are not men o' their words:
> They told me I was everything; 'tis a lie, I
> am not ague-proof.

At the top of the play, Lear is assailed by the voices of reason and good advice from three very different sources. He chooses to ignore all of them.

His youngest daughter, Cordelia, speaks straight from the heart. She will not pander to her father's narcissism, love of flattery and bullshit. She sees through her sisters' hypocrisy and treachery, and tries to warn her dad against them.

His loyal servant Kent sees that Lear is committing a fatal mistake in dumping his loyal daughter and splitting up his territory; it must eventuate in sibling rivalry and civil war.

His simple but wise fool sees into the depths of Lear's octogenarian folly and self-deceit. He foresees all too clearly the treachery of Goneril and Regan, and the price Lear will pay by abdicating all power and responsibility.

For me *King Lear* is the greatest of Shakespeare's plays – indeed, the greatest play ever written – but also the hardest to perform. It is almost impossible to bring off, such is the scope of its dystopian vision, the depths of its pain and cruelty, the emotional and psychological demands on the audience and its deconstruction of what we call civilised society. I have yet to see a performance that comes near to realising the play's challenges.

But by contemplating it we can learn life lessons beyond those of any philosophical or theological tract:

- Know when to step down. We all have a use-by date, no matter how grand we think we are.
- Prepare a workable succession plan.
- Don't play games with people's loyalty and affection.

- Deconstruct all flattery – what is its endgame?
- Listen to the voices of reason, wisdom and experience.
- Never act in rage, vengeance or the heat of the moment. That is simply self-indulgence. Give yourself time to cool down – and an exit strategy.
- Calculate reasonable expectations (Lear's were far too extravagant). How do they look from the other person's perspective?

What you do makes a difference, and you have to decide what kind of difference you want to make.

Jane Goodall

SHAKESPEARE ON RESILIENCE

Wise men ne'er sit and wail their loss,
But cheerly seek how to redress their harms.
Henry VI (Part III)

AMBITION

> For what profits a man if he gains the whole world but loses his soul?
> **Mark 8:36**

You don't have to believe in souls to get the point of the above quote. For 'soul' you can substitute 'self-respect', 'peace of mind' or some other commodity precious to you.

The point is that ambition can be a very destructive property. There's nothing wrong with ambition in itself; where would we be without it? We would never have put a man on the moon. There would have been no Roman Empire, Great Pyramid of Giza or Sistine Chapel. Every great human undertaking, every great industry or business, is sparked and fuelled by ambition.

The problems occur when ambition is misdirected away from the general good and towards self-aggrandisement. As Brutus says in *Julius Caesar*:

> The abuse of greatness is when it disjoins remorse from power.

Shakespeare doesn't mean 'remorse' in the way we hear it as 'regret'. He means something closer to 'empathy' or 'humanity'.

People who are overambitious are in danger of losing their humanity, ethical practice and common decency. Shakespeare often uses the word 'ambition' disapprovingly. The world he moved in was crammed with ambitious soldiers and aristocrats competing for honours and entertaining few scruples about wiping out any opposition. Heroes like Walter Raleigh and Francis Drake jostled for the queen's attention. Some jostled too hard, like Macbeth's 'vaulting ambition, which o'erleaps itself and falls on the other'. Such a one was Robert Devereux, Second Earl of Essex. He was the queen's favourite but overplayed his hand when in 1601 he staged a coup in an attempt to overthrow the government. He lost his head for his trouble.

Elsewhere in this book I scrutinised Julius Caesar and the ambition that proved to be his fatal flaw. But I keep asking myself the same question: why? What more did he want? Has ambition any limits? Caesar was already hailed as Rome's military hero. He had defeated Pompey in the Civil War and conquered Gaul, Britain, modern-day Belgium, Switzerland and the Netherlands. The Senate had awarded him no less than four Triumphs and made him dictator for life.

Yet still Caesar wanted more. Taking his cue from the Roman historians, Shakespeare suggests that Caesar wanted to dissolve the Republic, restore the monarchy and make himself king. He was already king in all but name, but seems to have craved the adulation and semi-divine status a crown would bestow on him.

Hitherto Caesar's ambition had been a huge asset to the Republic but now threatened its existence. What was in it for Caesar apart from a huge ego trip? (We are here, as always, talking about Shakespeare's Julius Caesar rather than the historical man himself; who can guess what his actual motives were?)

No other leader in Shakespeare is so out of touch with what's going on around him, the signs of conspiracy and discontent. Caesar is a shrewd judge of character but is overconfident of his status and invulnerability: he fears no one 'for always I am Caesar'.

Shakespeare's plays return again and again to the Cain and Abel theme of brothers pitted against each other – one driven by ambition and envy to destroy the other. We see it most notably in *King Lear* with the bastard Edmund plotting against his legitimate brother Edgar. In *Hamlet* Claudius poisons his brother, stealing his crown and his wife. The trilogy of plays dedicated to the reign of Henry VI depict the treachery and double-dealing of three brothers vying for the crown, with the bloodiest of the three coming out on top as Richard III.

But even the comedies are haunted by the shadow of fraternal skulduggery. In *As You Like It,* one brother supplants and banishes the other in order to become duke, and the same thing happens in *The Tempest.* Either Shakespeare found the story of Cain and Abel an affecting and useful dramatic trope or he was fascinated by the internecine conflicts of the great English families around him.

But the most intense and tragic exploration of ambition is found in *Macbeth*. As with Caesar, you'd think the Macbeths would be content with having *enough*. They are well established in terms of prestige and property – objects of universal admiration, praised by their king and fellow nobles. But there is a potent drop of ambition in both of them, which, let loose, runs like a poison through their veins. It runs more freely, almost uninhibited, through Lady Macbeth. With Macbeth it is blocked, initially, by scruples. But eventually, it takes full flood and destroys him.

What is the nature of this ambition? In the words of Lady Macbeth it is for 'solely sovereign sway and masterdom' – the excitement of supremacy. There is no pretence at doing it for 'the good of the country', to enhance justice, wellbeing or social reform – just the lust to dominate.

I guess the kind of ambition that drives Macbeth is neither strange nor unfamiliar to us. Australian politics over at least the last decade has given us a continuous soap opera of contenders bullying or grafting their way to the party leadership, while in the corporate or financial world you're not going to get far without a good strong dose of killer instinct. That instinct has always been accepted as a very 'male' thing, but over the last fifty or sixty years women have been demonstrating that they have much the same capability, to the shock and awe of the old boys' clubs.

So Lady Macbeth's ambition is no aberration. Queen Elizabeth herself had set a benchmark for female independence of spirit, and English women were regarded by Europeans as being remarkably free and outspoken. Nevertheless, Lady Macbeth feels that the horror of the murder she is about to commit (of the king no less) demands a rejection of her femininity:

>...Come, you spirits
>That tend on mortal thoughts, unsex me here;
>And fill me, from the crown to the toe, top-full
>Of direst cruelty ... Make thick my blood,

> ...
> Come to my woman's breasts
> And take my milk for gall, you murdering ministers.

At this point of the play her will is stronger than her husband's, and it is likely that Macbeth would have pulled back from assassinating King Duncan without her vehement insistence. But as the story progresses Macbeth becomes increasingly hard-hearted and single-minded, an isolated and paranoid figure who no longer needs his wife's complicity. Haunted by nightmares and insomnia, callously disposing of anyone who may prove to be a threat, he retreats into the dark cavern of his imagination, pinning all his hopes on the ambivalent prophecies of those three weird women who promised him the crown.

The first step in his undoing is his murder of Duncan, which is done in so botched a manner and so poorly covered up that it immediately arouses the suspicions of his fellow thanes, even as he tries to lay the blame on the king's sons Malcolm and Donalbain, who flee the country.

His best friend Banquo was present when the three women promised Macbeth a crown, but as you will remember they also promised Banquo that he would head a dynasty. The thought of this enrages Macbeth; he has committed regicide and damned himself, simply to make Banquo's children kings! So Banquo has to go. Macbeth plots the assassination of Banquo and his son Fleance – but Fleance escapes. The night of Banquo's death Macbeth throws a coronation banquet and all the thanes are bidden. Pretending ignorance of Banquo's fate, Macbeth proposes a toast to him, thereby conjuring up Banquo's ghost, which only Macbeth can see. His grotesque and horrified response further convinces the thanes of his guilt in the murders of both Duncan and Banquo.

The worthy Macduff has skipped the banquet and instead headed for England to summon back Malcolm and an English army to overthrow the tyrant. Learning of this, Macbeth orders the slaughter of Macduff's family and holes up in his castle of Dunsinane.

Meanwhile it has all been downhill for Lady Macbeth. Abandoned by her insomniac paranoid husband, she spirals into madness, driven by all that guilt she has suppressed for so long. Hers is a pathetic decline from a dazzling lady of high society to a shambling, muttering wraith – the rotten fruit born of ambition. Her suicide leaves Macbeth unmoved, apart from a mild surprise that he is no longer able to feel any kind of emotion. He suffers one last devastating shock when he realises that the women's prophecies, on which he had built his hopes, were hollow lies: they promised him he would be safe until the day Birnam forest marched on Dunsinane. He looks out the window to see the forest advancing on him – the trees chopped down and held by the English soldiers to conceal their numbers as they march.

They promised him no man 'born of woman' could harm him. Too late he is told that Macduff was not technically 'born', but delivered by caesarean. These are quibbles that mock his credulity. His head is cut off by Macduff and held up to the admiring crowd.

Watching the downfall of the Macbeths, we have to ask ourselves:

- What am I prepared to pay to make it to the top of the pile? Is the reward worth my sanity, my self-respect, my relationship, my reputation, my friendships?
- What credence should I give to flattering advice? What is the agenda of those who offer it? Why didn't I read the fine print? Who were those three weird women anyway? Was I being set up?
- When is enough? How do I weigh the extra prestige, salary, influence against what I already have? Will having more of those things make me any happier? I must weigh

what I have to gain against what I have to lose.

A story like that of the Macbeths urges us to maintain a balance between ambition and ethical behaviour. Life is pretty short, so what are your priorities? Who are the people, what are the things that most matter to you? Looking back on your life, how do you want to feel about what you've done? Will you be one of those people who, on their deathbed, says, 'I wish I'd spent less time at the office'?

I guess I've always been ambitious, perhaps crazily so – how else could I have dared to launch a theatre company on the smell of an oily rag not just once but twice? But I was never ambitious for the things that tempt some folks into showbiz: I didn't give a cuss for the fame and the glitz, and I've never been much concerned about money. My big ambition was to work in the world's best plays, if possible with some of the world's best people. That ambition has never waned and has prevented me from becoming cynical or jaded about a profession that, for some people, turns out to be hollow and unsatisfying.

***

Another Shakespearean protagonist whose ambition drives him to seize the crown (though not in so bloody a fashion as Macbeth) is Henry Bolingbroke, who overthrows his cousin Richard II as I touched on earlier.

Bolingbroke is an exemplar of medieval chivalry who is unjustly banished and robbed of his estates by the impetuous king. Outraged, Bolingbroke raises an army of sympathisers and invades England to reclaim his own. He forces Richard to abdicate and claims the crown for himself. Richard is conveniently murdered in prison and, although Bolingbroke professes his innocence, he is haunted by the memory of his cousin's murder and, like Macbeth, is plagued by insomnia.

Bolingbroke, now Henry IV, finds little joy in his exalted status, realising too late that 'uneasy lies the head that wears a crown'.

***

For a portrait of naked ambition, unapologetic and devoid of moral scruples, we need look no further than Richard III (you may recall him from the earlier discussion on physical courage in times of crisis). At least Henry IV did not set out deliberately to usurp his cousin, but was led to do so incrementally. Nor did he directly order Richard II's murder. And Macbeth had the excuse of supernatural urgings and his wife's domineering personality driving him to assassinate King Duncan.

But Richard, Duke of Gloucester, is, from the moment we meet him, hell-bent on hacking his way to the throne, bumping off anyone who gets in the way. He is composed of treachery, cunning and malice, and is driven by a lust to domineer the world, which, since childhood, has spurned and derided him because of his physical deformity:

> Then, since this world affords no joy to me
> But to command, to check, to o'erbear such
> As are of better person than myself,
> I'll make my heaven to dream upon the crown,
> And, whiles I live, to account this world but hell,
> Until my misshaped trunk that bears this head
> Be round impaled with a glorious crown.
> ...
> Why, I can smile, and murder whiles I smile,
> And cry 'Content!' to that which grieves my heart,
> And wet my cheeks with artificial tears,
> And frame my face to all occasions.

Having proved himself to be a brutal warrior during the Wars of the Roses, Richard chafes for action once peace is declared and starts plotting the downfall of his elder brothers, King Edward and George, Duke of Clarence. He concocts what we now call fake news to convince Edward that George is plotting against him. George is thrown into the Tower of London, where Richard has him murdered. When the king submits to illness, Richard kidnaps his young sons, who are also murdered in the tower.

He marries the young Lady Anne for political reasons, but soon has her dispatched in order to make a more advantageous alliance. Various nobles, including his closest buddy Buckingham, are picked off one by one if they show any opposition to his tyranny. Eventually, the remaining nobles fly from his side to join Henry, Earl of Richmond, who defeats Richard at the Battle of Bosworth and declares himself Henry VII.

Throughout the course of Shakespeare's *Richard III*, Richard is a witty, cynical and vastly entertaining protagonist. But the murder of the little princes in the Tower of London drains away any admiration the audience might have had for him. His insolent carapace finally cracks, and the night before the fatal battle he is haunted by the ghosts of his victims. Like Macbeth he suffers the pangs of guilt and insomnia, and faces the inevitability of his eternal damnation:

>My conscience hath a thousand several tongues,
>And every tongue brings in a several tale,
>And every tale condemns me for a villain.
>Perjury, perjury in the highest degree;
>Murder, stern murder in the direst degree;
>All several sins, all used in each degree
>Throng to the bar, crying all 'Guilty! Guilty!'
>I shall despair. There is no creature loves me;
>And if I die, no soul will pity me.

But come the dawn he puts on a brave face and rallies his troops, a flamboyant and charismatic buccaneer to the end:

>Go, gentlemen, every man unto his charge.
>Let not our babbling dreams affright our souls.
>Conscience is but a word that cowards use,
>Devis'd at first to keep the strong in awe.
>Our strong arms be our conscience, swords our law.
>March on, join bravely, let us to it pell-mell;
>If not to heaven, then hand in hand to hell.

Can we learn any useful lessons from the notorious Richard III? Perhaps all we can do is hold him as a template of forewarning when observing the operations of leaders on the international stage, in our own federal and state politics, and in corporations and professions including the law and the Church.

Whenever we suspect there are deals being done in bad faith; whenever malicious fake news is being bruited; whenever we suspect plotting and cheating by those aspiring to the top; whenever we suspect we are being used as tools in a crafty political exercise; whenever we sniff hypocrisy, lies, cover-ups, bribery and corruption; whenever the honeyed words of an orator strike us as hollow and self-seeking; whenever we suspect the demonisation of good and honest people; whenever a leader's promises are vague, ill-defined, too good to be true – at such times we might say to ourselves, 'Ah, yes! Richard III!'

True hope is swift, and flies with swallow's wings:
Kings it makes gods, and meaner creatures kings.
Richard III

SHAKESPEARE ON INITIATIVE

Men at some time are masters of their fates:
The fault, dear Brutus, is not in our stars,
But in ourselves, that we are underlings.
Julius Caesar

CHARISMA, CONFIDENCE AND HUMILITY

Optimism is the faith that leads to achievement.
Helen Keller

Ask the person in the street to name the qualities that make a successful leader and one of the first words they'll likely reach for is 'charisma'. It's a dangerous commodity, charisma: Hitler, Stalin and Mussolini had it in buckets; you can see it in the rapturous faces at their mass rallies.

It's also a commodity that can readily be manufactured, or at least enhanced, by a team of spin doctors, speechwriters, makeup artists and costume designers. Charisma does not depend on great physical attributes: Hitler was as plain as a doorknob; Napoleon was short; and lanky, ungainly Lincoln had a high thin voice. They made up for it with willpower, stamina and forceful personalities.

To these attributes admirable leaders will add *authenticity*. They will be trustworthy, inspiring, visionary and have a way with words.

They will have a generosity of spirit and a sense of destiny. They will give you their full and undivided attention. Add all these together and you might end up with something like charisma.

Henry V is the most charismatic of Shakespeare's studies in leadership. And he dies young, before things start going pear-shaped, as they do for Mark Antony, that other charismatic leader.

Henry projects a tireless enthusiasm and belief in his mission. Under all the bravado there is a cool resilience that refuses to crack under strain. His optimism is contagious and inclusive. He listens to his followers and notes their concerns. (I believe that one of the skills a leader must develop is inclusiveness, the skill of empowering everyone in the team.)

Henry shows genuine concern for his officers and calls each by name. Individuals are singled out and made to feel highly valued. He is confident enough to send himself up and play the fool for the French princess in order to charm her and win her hand.

Henry's personal bravery and prowess on the battlefield are legendary, and he always leads from the front as an identifiable target. (Compare this with his more cautious – one might say cowardly – father, who had a number of knights disguised in the royal armour to distract attention from himself.)

Henry V has all the charisma missing in his father. Henry Bolingbroke, Henry IV, is tough and ambitious, but once he has attained his goal he becomes aloof and withdrawn, mistaking arrogance for authority.

Surrounded by foes who resent his deposition of Richard II, and rebellious stirrings in Wales and Scotland, Bolingbroke's biggest mistake is to snub his chief supporters. (Lesson: always acknowledge those who have helped you get to the top. You have nothing to lose by saying thank you.)

He attempts to give his son, Prince Harry (soon to become Henry V), some points in public relations: he castigates him for being 'so stale and cheap to vulgar company', for hanging around with petty crims in pubs and brothels, whereas:

> By being seldom seen, I could not stir
> But, like a comet, I was wonder'd at;
> That men would tell their children 'This is he';
> Others would say 'Where? Which is Bolingbroke?'
> And then I ... dressed myself in such humility
> That I did pluck allegiance from men's hearts,

> Loud shouts and salutations from their mouths,
>
> ...
>
> Thus did keep my person fresh and new.

In other words, Bolingbroke's charisma is all an act, a performance: 'dressed myself in such humility'. Whatever charisma or charm he might once have had in order to rally followers to his cause, Bolingbroke loses it once he ascends the throne. He becomes gloomy and morose, haunted with guilt over the murder of his cousin, Richard II. His misery is compounded by the delinquent antics of his eldest son, Prince Harry. Bolingbroke lacks the personal and moral authority to defy his critics and bring the rebellious factions together.

Climbing to the top of the heap is one thing; another is to hold your balance once you're up there.

Is charisma essential to good leadership? Apparently not. Many successful leaders in commerce, industry and politics are notably lacking charisma.

Some people are born leaders; most have to work at it. Leadership is a skill that can be learned. Throughout my career I have made a point of studying the leadership qualities of the many directors I have worked with. Some have been tyrannical (effective in the short term but deadening in the long run); some too compliant, letting the noisiest person in the room suck up all the air. The best have been the sincerely collaborative, secure enough in themselves to give everyone a voice without feeling threatened. Most stage directors never get to see their fellow directors at work. But as an actor I have had the chance to see firsthand many different directions and learn what to use and what to avoid.

Henry V works hard at cultivating his image. He witnesses the failure of his father's attempt to gain authority – by remaining stern, aloof and inflexible. Young Harry decides on a different course of action. As a teenager he avoids the court and most of his princely duties, preferring to spend his time in the pubs and brothels of London's Eastcheap in company of the riotous, warm-hearted Jack Falstaff and his gang of petty thieves. As well as enjoying sowing his wild oats, Hal is working at a carefully calibrated game plan. He is getting to know the ways of his future subjects – who they are and how they live. He is developing 'the common touch'.

Two other of Shakespeare's people with enormous charisma are Mark Antony and Cleopatra; but it avails them little as leaders because it seduces them away from any sense of responsibility and into a fantasy existence of acting out their own celebrity.

Mark Antony's early career defines him as a favourite indulged and trusted by Julius Caesar. As we saw earlier, his mentor's assassination galvanises him, partly out of genuine grief and outrage, partly out of a desire for revenge on the assassins and partly out of the possible opportunity for his own advancement.

After Brutus and Cassius are defeated and forced to commit suicide, Antony and Caesar's nephew Octavius team up with Marcus Lepidus to rule as triumvirs of the Republic. Antony soon tires of the plodding Lepidus, who is given the flick, leaving two ambitious men to rule the empire between them – an explosive situation. (Think of Facebook's Mark Zuckerberg and Eduardo Saverin or Apple's Steve Jobs and John Sculley.)

Antony's attention is soon focused on Cleopatra, the beguiling Queen of Egypt who accommodated the Roman takeover of her empire by seducing Julius Caesar and having a son by him, thus securing protection for herself and, to some extent, the remains of her kingdom. She now tilts at Antony, contriving an extension of her privileged position.

In next to no time Antony is wildly in lust with her and his passion is reciprocated. In terms of ego, energy, sensuality and recklessness, these two are perfectly matched. The whole world can go hang while they indulge themselves in an exhilarating and tempestuous affair.

Octavius is furious that Antony is not shouldering his share of the burden of empire and is whiling away his career in the arms of 'a gypsy whore'. Various efforts are made to patch up their quarrel, but Antony and Octavius are on a collision course and put their armies and battle fleets on standby. The night before their climactic battle, instead of soberly preparing for action, Antony and Cleopatra call their captains to celebrate 'one more gaudy night' of drinking and revelling. It's almost as if they are willing themselves to lose.

Following their inevitable defeat, Antony and Cleopatra both commit suicide, leaving Octavius in sole control. He soon installs himself as Augustus, Rome's first emperor. The great Republic is well and truly dead.

The charisma that attaches itself to Antony and Cleopatra stems from their personal magnetism and the devotion they inspire. Both are moody, wilful and selfish, but they have a zest for life and a generosity of spirit that stands in stark contrast to the cold-blooded, pragmatic Octavius. Antony and Cleopatra are capable of displaying great affection and generosity to their followers. When Antony's closest friend Enobarbus deserts him and switches his allegiance to Octavius, Antony is saddened rather than vengeful. He sends all of Enobarbus's war booty to him along with a note of affection and forgiveness. Mortified and overcome with grief, Enobarbus kills himself.

When Cleopatra decides to kill herself rather than fall into the hands of Octavius, her ladies insist on dying with her. That is the kind of adoration these legendary lovers inspire.

Speaking of the dead Antony, Cleopatra says:
> O, wither'd is the garland of the war,
> The soldier's pole is fallen! Young boys and girls
> Are level now with men. The odds is gone,
> And there is nothing left remarkable
> Beneath the visiting moon
> ...
> His legs bestrid the ocean; his rear'd arm
> Crested the world. His voice was propertied
> As all the tuned spheres, and that to friends;
> But when he meant to quail and shake the orb,
> He was as rattling thunder. For his bounty,
> There was no winter in't; an autumn 'twas

> That grew the more by reaping. His delights
> Were dolphin-like: they show'd his back above
> The element they lived in...

Wrapped in their own charisma, Antony and Cleopatra dwell on a plane detached from reality.

The main lesson we can take from watching Antony's rise and fall is to note how vital it is to know how to cope with success and celebrity. It's one thing to make it to the top but then you need the sobriety, restraint and cunning to stay there.

If you get the top job you will inevitably be prey to sycophants, flatterers and opportunists looking to share the limelight or push you out of it.

To handle this you need to stay level-headed and maintain a sense of humour as well as a genuine humility. Brutus muses that:

> 'Tis a common proof
> That lowliness is young ambition's ladder,
> Whereto the climber upward turns his face;
> But when he once attains the utmost round,
> He then unto the ladder turns his back,
> Looks in the clouds, scorning the base degrees

By which he did ascend.

To me, humility means having a genuine assessment of your own worth while acknowledging superior qualities in others. Remember where you came from, how you got to where you are and who helped you to get there.

***

From Shakespeare's representation of charisma and confidence, we can take away these points:
- Don't get carried away with your own charisma. Don't believe your own publicity.
- Don't think you made it all on your own. Remember the people who helped you get there. Acknowledge them and remain grateful.
- 'Charisma' is a word too freely f lung about, like 'genius'. It's not necessary to possess charisma to be an effective leader, but it can help if it attracts the attention and the team you want about you.
- Once you've made it to the top you need the self-discipline to stay there. Antony boozes away an empire. Remote from his power base and living a life of self-indulgent luxury, he fails to keep an eye on the

competition and doesn't see Octavius coming up behind him.
- **The top job demands your full attention, awareness and dexterity.**

Imagination is more important than knowledge, because knowledge is limited but imagination circles the world.
Albert Einstein

SHAKESPEARE ON WISDOM

The fool doth think he is wise, but the wise man knows himself to be a fool.
Twelfth Night

INTEGRITY AND HUMANITY

Success isn't about how much money you make – it's about the difference you make in people's lives.
Michelle Obama

Do what you know in your heart to be right, for you'll be criticised anyway.
Eleanor Roosevelt

Like most professions, showbiz is full of people who have 'clawed their way to the top'. Some of them settle down once they've got there and turn out okay. But I've always heeded the old adage: 'Be nice to people who are on the way up, because you may meet them again when you're on the way down.' In the bad old days Hollywood and Broadway were full of producers who screwed, in every possible way, people desperate to work. Strong unionism and the Me Too movement have put a stop to a lot of that – misbehaviour can now shut down a show and destroy a career overnight. Theatre is a fragile industry that depends heavily on goodwill, generosity, absolute trust and integrity.

It's not easy, scanning a list of Shakespeare's male protagonists, to find a man of unimpeachable integrity. Many claim to have it, but their flaws are soon revealed. One who comes closest is Brutus in *Julius Caesar*. Elsewhere in this book I examined Brutus's shortcomings, but there is no doubting his moral integrity. He has grave misgivings about the future of the Roman Republic in the light of Caesar's dictatorial ambitions. (Caesar is already dictator for life, but wants more. It's interesting to compare his ambition with that of Vladimir Putin and Xi Jinping, who are obviously of like mind.)

As we know, Brutus is hugely reluctant to join the plot to kill Caesar, especially as the man has been his friend and patron. But he is persuaded (or persuades himself) that the assassination is for the greater good.

Even when things go badly awry, Brutus is adamant that he has done the right thing. His integrity is also recognised by Mark Antony, his nemesis, who pronounces over Brutus's corpse:

> This was the noblest Roman of them all.
> All the conspirators save only he
> Did that they did in envy of great Caesar;
> He only, in a general honest thought
> And common good to all, made one of them.
> His life was gentle; and the elements

So mingled in him that Nature might stand up
And say to all the world, 'This was a man!'

All of Shakespeare's other male protagonists are flawed in some way. In *Measure for Measure* Angelo finds that the privilege of absolute power corrupts his customary rectitude and seduces him into committing grave abuse of his office.

Othello is betrayed by his pride and jealousy and Hamlet becomes so disillusioned and callous that he can treacherously dispatch his old friends Rosencrantz and Guildenstern with a shrug.

With the leading men thus compromised, we have to look to the second rank to find the men of solid moral fibre. Macduff is Macbeth's opposite number and nemesis. He is honest, loyal and incorruptible. He has the acumen and courage to question Macbeth's cover-up of Duncan's murder and the pluckiness to travel to England and seek foreign aid to overthrow the Scottish tyrant.

In *King Lear* the loyal Kent is banished for speaking his mind, but has the compassion and generosity to come back in disguise to aid his mad old master as best he can. His self-sacrifice is matched by that of Edgar, who also adopts a disguise to save and protect his father, Gloucester. Neither man expects thanks or recognition. They are driven purely by pity, kindness and a sense of duty. They give us reassurance that in a world of violence, evil and selfishness there are those who will stand up, protest and risk their lives for decency's sake. We still need that reassurance today. It has been inspiring, but also heartbreaking, to watch the young political activist Joshua Wong's defiance of China's brutal takeover of Hong Kong. One fears he's fighting for a lost cause. He reminds me of the anonymous man standing before the tanks in the Tiananmen Square protests of 1989. Greta Thunberg, in her furious denunciation of climate change complacency, is another inspirational leader of the next generation.

Surrounded by treachery and intrigue, Hamlet finds that Horatio is his one true friend. He is a man of humble background and Hamlet's fellow student. He is always there but in the background, ready to advise, support and protect. Unlike almost every other character in the play, Horatio has no personal agenda or selfish motive. He is there simply to serve as a friend. In a moment of intense emotion Hamlet says to him:

> Dost thou hear?
> Since my dear soul was mistress of her choice
> And could of men distinguish her election

> She hath seal'd thee for herself; for thou hast been
> As one, in suff'ring all that suffers nothing;
> A man that Fortune's buffets and rewards
> Hast taken with equal thanks; and blest are those
> Whose blood and judgement are so well co-mingled
> That they are not a pipe for Fortune's finger
> To sound what stop she please. Give me that man
> That is not passion's slave, and I will wear him
> In my heart's core, ay, in my heart of heart,
> As I do thee.

I can't imagine a more eloquent tribute to integrity.

Apart from this handful of male characters, we need to turn to Shakespeare's women to find models of complete integrity.

Their author faced a tough challenge in creating their roles because, as women were not allowed on stage at the time, the female roles had to be played by men and boys.

His earliest female roles are pretty tough cookies and you can picture male actors swaggering in them: the tomboy Joan of Arc and ferocious Queen Margaret of *Henry VI;* Tamora the vindictive Queen of the Goths in *Titus Andronicus*. But roles become more feminised as he launches into the Comedies with lusty battle-of-the-sexes scenarios like *The Taming of the Shrew* and *Much Ado About Nothing*. In both these plays there is an invigorating tension between two well-matched protagonists. An entertaining war of wits and fiery temperaments ensues as man and woman try to thrash out a contract that is acceptable to them both.

In succumbing to marriage the women in these plays sacrifice some degree of independence, but the deals they strike with their partners are workable in the context of a loving relationship.

In *Love's Labour's Lost* four very smart young women totally befuddle their aspiring lovers and teach them how shallow is their concept of true love. Rosalind undertakes a similar mission in *As You Like It*, educating all the love-smitten wooers in the play as to the nature of true love: responsibility, patience, equality and self-sacrifice.

Rosalind is one of those young Shakespearean heroines trying to find a voice and an authoritative role in a male-dominated society. The only way she can do this is to get into male costume and challenge the men at their own game. Viola does the same thing in *Twelfth Night*; Portia does it in *The Merchant of Venice*, Silvia in *The Two Gentlemen of Verona* and Imogen in *Cymbeline* .

Portia is the most notable example of a woman determined to rule the roost. The merchant Antonio has a crush on young Bassanio. His passion is unrequited but Bassanio needs money to woo the wealthy heiress Portia. Lacking the present means, Antonio grudgingly borrows the sum from his archenemy, Shylock the Jewish moneylender. When he defaults on the loan, Shylock is permitted by law to take his life.

Realising Bassanio's dilemma, Portia disguises herself as a male doctor of law and is able to outwit Shylock in court, save Antonio's life and thereby break the bond of obligation Antonio holds over her lover.

For all her conventional feminine charm, Portia is a single-minded and tough negotiator. She has the perspicacity to realise the nature of Antonio's feelings for Bassanio, and the wit and daring to undertake a course of action that is entirely outside the bounds of the law.

I once sought the opinion of two judges as to Portia's behaviour. One was highly critical: 'She's making a monkey out of the law; she's impersonating a lawyer and she isn't even a man!' The other was more sympathetic: 'She uses the law to its proper end – to save the life of someone pursued by a mischievous litigant.'

In the Comedies, women find a voice and authority by adopting a false male persona and using their wit, charm and female tenderness to lead the menfolk to an awareness of their follies and a better understanding of successful male/female coexistence and interdependence.

But in the great late Tragedies and so-called Romances, Shakespeare allows his female characters to become the moral authority, the wise and compassionate characters who are frequently the victims of male blindness and stupidity, but rise above their suffering and force their male counterparts into humiliated contrition.

Theatrical tradition has in the past portrayed *Othello*'s Desdemona as a meek and submissive sacrificial lamb. The evidence is to the contrary.

She is better seen as an idealistic and adventurous teenager who, born into Venetian aristocracy, defies her father and elopes with Othello, a middle-aged Black man – she's hardly a shrinking violet. Othello is duped by his evil subordinate Iago into believing that Desdemona is having an affair with the young lieutenant Cassio. Iago is driven by malice, envy and a degree of racial hatred in his plot to destroy Othello; Desdemona is simply collateral damage.

Desdemona is strong but inexperienced in the ways of the world. More experienced and equally strong is her companion Emilia, Iago's wife. Emilia does her best to deflect Othello's jealous rage, and her anger blazes when she finds that Othello has murdered his wife at Iago's instigation. She first rounds on Othello:

Oh, the more angel she,
And you the blacker devil!
...
Oh gull! Oh dolt!
As ignorant as dirt!

And then she publicly accuses and condemns Iago before he stabs her to death.

As brave and honest as Emilia is, Desdemona has the last word when it comes to heroism. Even though Othello has slain her she rallies for a moment to save his life. Realising that her husband has been gulled by a villain, she wants to save him from execution. When Emilia asks 'O, who hath done this deed?' Desdemona replies, with her last breath:

Nobody. I myself. Farewell.
Commend me to my kind lord. Oh, farewell!

Such heroic self-sacrifice is truly heartbreaking. It certainly is for Othello, who kills himself on the spot.

Cordelia is another young heroine who is sometimes undercooked in stage presentations. She is no shrinking violet either, but a perceptive, honest and outspoken young woman for whom integrity is more important than status or material security.

Her octogenarian father, King Lear, is looking forward to a happy retirement, but one that retains all the perks. As noted earlier, he will divide his kingdom among his three daughters and spend time with each of them, attended by his personal retinue of a hundred knights. The best parcel of land will go to the daughter who loves him the most (already privately earmarked for his favourite, Cordelia).

The two older siblings, Goneril and Regan, try to outdo each other with flattering protestations of affection but Cordelia refuses to play the game, seeing it as an irresponsible ego trip based on hypocrisy. Furious, Lear divides his kingdom between Goneril and Regan and disowns Cordelia. Fortunately the King of France is on the spot and takes her for his wife.

Her older sisters strip Lear of all his followers and he ends up a lonely lunatic figure wandering in the wilderness. And this is where

Cordelia's integrity kicks in: instead of saying 'I told you so', she leads a French army to Britain to face her treacherous sisters and save her father.

Unfortunately she fails. Her army is defeated, she is hanged and her father dies with her in his arms. But something has been achieved. Goneril and Regan have also destroyed each other and now the blighted landscape is clear for a fresh start. Despite its apocalyptic vision, *King Lear* does display the green shoots of hope.

First among these is the devotion, integrity and self-sacrifice of Cordelia. She has no time for sham protestations; she calls out falsehood and hypocrisy; she challenges her foolish father's system of values, forgives his outrageous treatment of her and risks her life to save him.

Cordelia's outstanding virtues are honesty, integrity, perceptiveness, outspokenness, courage, generosity, compassion and forgiveness. None of these should be regarded as 'soft' virtues; indeed they have been demonstrated by some of history's strongest leaders, such as Abraham Lincoln and Nelson Mandela.

Happily she is not alone in this bleak, harsh world that Shakespeare dreams up. There is the faithful Kent, also banished for speaking out, but who returns in disguise to serve and protect his master. Lear's faithful Fool also sticks by him as long as he is able, nagging him, warning him, trying to open his eyes to the lies and deceit all around him. And finally we have Edgar, that faithful son in a parallel narrative, trying to save his aged father from a treacherous brother. Without these exemplars of selfless integrity, *King Lear* would present an unmitigated vision of despair. At least Lear is brought to his senses and an understanding of his mere mortality, and is reconciled to his faithful and forgiving daughter.

***

One of Shakespeare's last plays is *The Winter's Tale,* which, on the surface, has all the charm and absurdity of a fairytale; but deeper down it has a lot to say about pain and loss, cruelty and forgiveness and the miracle of regeneration.

Leontes, King of Sicily, is struck with a fit of mad jealousy and suspects his pregnant wife Hermione is having an affair with his best friend Polixenes, King of Bohemia. He orders his faithful servant Camillo to poison Polixenes, but Camillo tips off Polixenes and the two of them flee to Bohemia.

Leontes now suspects that everyone is plotting against his life. Hermione is thrown into prison and her newborn daughter handed over to the aged courtier Antigonus with instructions to abandon her in some desert place. He leaves her on the shore of Bohemia, where she is discovered by an old shepherd who adopts her as his own.

Hermione, meanwhile, is put on public trial and defies Leontes' insane imaginings. Her speech to the court is a model of dignity, moderation, rationality and self-respect.

Hauled from the prison where she has just recently given birth, and forced to stand for trial in the open marketplace, she calmly refutes all Leontes' crazy accusations and lists his abuses, concluding:

> Now, my liege,
> Tell me what blessings I have here alive
> That I should fear to die. Therefore proceed.
> But yet hear this – mistake me not: no life,
> I prize it not a straw, but for mine honour,
> Which I would free – if I shall be condemned
> Upon surmises, all proofs sleeping else
> But what your jealousies awake, I tell you
> 'Tis rigour and not law.

Before she can be sentenced, a messenger arrives from the Oracle of Delphi proclaiming the innocence of Hermione and Polixenes, condemning Leontes and warning he will die without an heir if his baby daughter is not found.

Leontes now commits the ultimate blasphemy in refuting the words of the Oracle.

He is punished immediately with news of the death of his little prince, who has died of grief for his mother's distress. Hermione swoons and is taken away. Leontes is devastated with grief and guilt, which is increased tenfold when Hermione's attendant Paulina rushes back in and announces that Hermione too is dead. Paulina sheets all woe home to Leontes:

> Thy tyranny,
>
> Together working with thy jealousies...
> ...
> O think what they have done
> And then run mad indeed, stark mad...
> ...a fool, inconstant,
> And damnable ungrateful...
> O thou tyrant,
> ...betake thee
> To nothing but despair.

Now quite numb with grief, Leontes undertakes to live a life of monk-like penitence, and visit every day the tombs of his wife and son under the watchful eye of Paulina.

We then skip forward sixteen years and find ourselves in Bohemia, where the abandoned baby, Princess Perdita, has grown to be an attractive young lady in the cottage of the homely shepherd. She catches the eye of Prince Florizel, son of Polixenes, but when he proposes marriage to her his furious father commands him to have nothing to do with these peasants. The young couple elope to Sicily to seek the protection of King Leontes, whom they know to have been the boyhood friend of Polixenes. The old shepherd accompanies them and is able to prove that Perdita is the long-lost daughter of Leontes and Hermione.

Paulina promises to compound their joy by showing them a statue of Hermione she has kept hidden for sixteen years. The onlookers are amazed by the veracity of the 'statue', but when it comes alive and takes Leontes by the hand, they realise how completely Paulina has stage-managed the whole affair: protecting Hermione and putting Leontes through a process of contrition and healing that is brought to fruition when his daughter comes of age.

The only shadow over the general rejoicing is the memory of the little prince who died of grief, reminding us that not every fairytale has a perfectly happy ending.

The Winter's Tale gives us female characters who far outweigh the men when it comes to integrity, forgiveness, temperance, humility, courage, patience and rational thinking. Both Leontes and Polixenes demonstrate their tyranny in their abuse of power and refusal to listen to wise counsel. Like Lear they are trapped in their roles of autocratic patriarchs, answerable to no one.

Looking back over Shakespeare's female characters, we can see that:
- Leadership is about more than traditional 'male' attributes like bravado, forcefulness, teambuilding and so on.
- Leadership also entails perseverance, tenacity, wit, diplomacy, flexibility and an acute understanding of other people's agendas.
- Leadership has room for generosity, understanding, kindness, compassion and forgiveness.
- When you encounter a seemingly immovable obstacle, you don't need to dash yourself against it. Patience, wit and invention might show you there's a way around it.
- A bit of daring and a bit of chutzpah can carry you quite a long way.
- Playfulness is an attractive quality in a leader. Not everything needs to be taken with the same degree of seriousness.

- Pick your battles.
- Leadership calls for courage, integrity and adherence to truth.

Howcan we encourage integrity and humanity in our leaders? And how can we translate this range of skills and attributes illustrated by Shakespeare's female characters into a modern leader, such as a CEO? We should expect that a good CEO will:

- perceive others' strengths and weaknesses, and know how to accommodate or compensate for them
- know that listening is an important attribute of a leader
- allow others to question or challenge their ideas and not regard it as mutiny
- know that praising people, acknowledging their achievements and complimenting them in public provides the best incentive
- understand the necessity of constantly thanking and acknowledging donors, corporate partners and individual supporters (you can't say 'Thank you' too often)
- do their best to develop their people skills in terms of empathy, care and concern for all members of staff (a good CEO knows that a happy staff is a more productive one)
- project a positive, cheerful optimism at all times, even under stress, because they know

that hissy fits, tantrums and yelling at people earn only disrespect and contempt
- not play favourites, not adopt a secretive air and not appear brusque or disinterested in others' opinions
- know how destructive it is to choke communication, to silo people, to micromanage them, to seek to divide and rule and have people at odds with each other
- live the values of courage, integrity and authenticity.

If you don't risk anything, you risk even more.
Erica Jong

SHAKESPEARE ON THE THRILL OF LEADERSHIP

Things won are done; joy's soul lies in the doing.
Troilus and Cressida

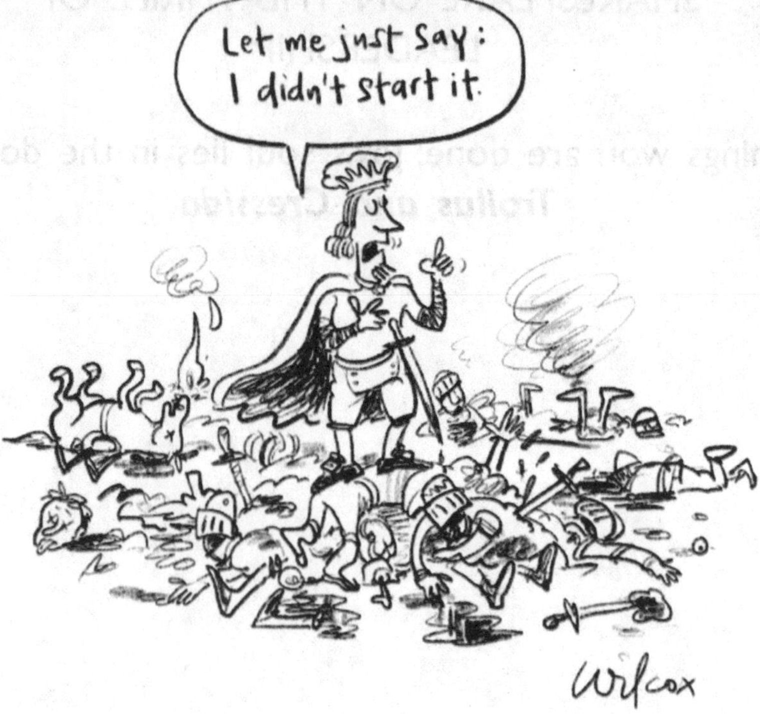
Let me just say:
I didn't start it.
Wilcox

AFTERWORD

Let's go off
And bear us like the time.
The Two Noble Kinsmen

I began writing this book before the advent of COVID-19. As the coronavirus has raged its way around the world, many of our accepted ideas and institutions have come under threat. We have watched our economies teeter on the brink, seen unemployment figures soar and businesses collapse. Flaws in infrastructure (for instance in our aged care system) have been exposed. We have been confronted with a host of social problems including the poor health and prison incarceration rates in Indigenous communities, and the discrepancy between the inflated salaries of some executives and the grinding poverty of those at the bottom of the heap – all of this against the background of a looming climate change catastrophe and its impact on food and water resources, its environmental devastation and the loss of flora and fauna. Ideological warfare has taken to the streets and been violently suppressed in several countries including The United States. And there is a disturbing escalation of tensions between superpowers America and China.

Huge challenges confront tomorrow's leaders, among them the eradication of worldwide poverty and the implementation of universal education, which in themselves would help mitigate many of the problems indicated above.

Pundits keep telling us that when this pandemic is over (if it ever is) we will find ourselves in a different world to the one we know now. Nobody is able or willing yet to tell us what this world will be like. But the qualities of good leadership I have enumerated in this book will hold good, with a special emphasis on originality, flexibility and the skill to forecast the effects of decisions taken. Tomorrow's leaders will need to put an extra emphasis on generosity, compassion and empathy if they are going to inspire people. They will need to be articulate, courageous and resilient.

Does Shakespeare reflect on this? Most certainly. All his great Tragedies end in the devastation and grief caused by ambition, malice, greed and arrogance. But there is always a coda permitting someone resourceful and clear-sighted to pick up the pieces and establish a new generation of hope and renewal – be it Edgar in *King Lear*, Fortinbras in *Hamlet*, Malcolm in *Macbeth* or Richmond in *Richard III*:

> RICHMOND: God, if thy will be so,
> Enrich the time to come with smooth-faced peace,
> With smiling plenty and fair prosperous days.

But is that just sentimentality, the desire for a fairytale ending? *No.* It is profoundly necessary. We *must* be optimistic. There's no point being otherwise. We must have faith in the next generation and its capability to set things right. They are already giving us every reason to hope, to be inspired and to believe they can do it.

Today's leaders have the obligation to look after our next generation – to give them every possible nurture and encouragement, every opportunity – because the future of the world is in their hands. Necessarily they will see the world differently. They will have new solutions, new aspirations.

Each of Shakespeare's Tragedies heralds the arrival of a potential healer and inspirational leader. None of them underestimates the task ahead of them, but they are all prepared to take up the challenge. So must we.

ACKNOWLEDGEMENTS

During my years with Bell Shakespeare, I established a friendship with one of its longest-serving board members, David Pumphrey, an executive search consultant and partner in Heidrick ... Struggles. Several years ago David invited both me and James Evans, an actor and educator with Bell Shakespeare, to join him in addressing conferences in Southeast Asia on Shakespeare's insights into leadership and governance. That experience inspired many of the ideas contained in this book, and I thank David and James for their valuable input.

I am deeply grateful to my editor, Alexandra Payne, for her scrupulous revision of the manuscript and her many elegant suggestions as to its structure and clarity, and to all at Pantera Press. I am also thrilled with the contribution of the priceless Cathy Wilcox.

John Bell is one of the nation's most illustrious theatre personalities. Award-winning actor, acclaimed director, risk-taking impresario and torch-bearing educationalist, Bell has been a key figure in shaping the nation's theatrical identity as we know it over the past fifty years.

As co-founder of Nimrod Theatre Company, Bell presented many productions of landmark

Australian plays, and in 1990, he took on an even greater challenge, founding The Bell Shakespeare Company.

Bell's unique contribution to national culture has been recognised by many bodies. He is an Officer of the Order of Australia and the Order of the British Empire; has an Honorary Doctorate of Letters from the Universities of Sydney, New South Wales and Newcastle; and was recognised in 1997 by the National Trust of Australia as one of Australia's Living Treasures.

As an actor and director, he has many awards including two Helpmann Awards for Best Actor (*Richard III,* 2002 and *As You Like It,* 2015), a Producers and Directors Guild Award for Lifetime Achievement and the JC Williamson Award (2009) for extraordinary contribution to Australia's live entertainment industry.

'To thine own self be true, and it must follow, as the night the day, thou canst not then be false to any man.'
Hamlet

'Shows hope is not dead by a long shot.'
Weekly Times

JESS SCULLY

GLIMPSES OF UTOPIA

REAL IDEAS FOR A FAIRER WORLD

'*Glimpses of Utopia* provided me the rarest thing in these grim times: hope.'
Benjamin Law

'Jess Scully has scoured the world for the best ideas to fix this mess we're in.'
Jess Hill, *See What You Made Me Do*

BACK COVER MATERIAL

How are we to endure this global leadership drought?

There's a reason we often use the word 'Shakespearean' to describe dramatic times: William Shakespeare is our best analyst of human behaviour and motivation. A man well acquainted with turmoil, he produced works bristling with wit, profound empathy and a deep understanding of the best and worst of our nature. His words still ring with relevance today; they might just contain some of the answers we're looking for.

Australians are weary of the farcical spectacle of mid-term prime ministers being shoved through the revolving door, scandalous failures of governance in financial institutions and the moral abyss in Church stewardship. Throughout the mess of Brexit, chaotic unpredictability of the Trump administration and Covid-19 – the gravest leadership challenge since World War II – stable, reliable, sensible leadership has been in short supply.

Having spent a great deal of the last seventy-something years studying, performing and directing Shakespeare's plays, John Bell has absorbed timeless lessons in life, character and leadership from the Bard – and put these to good use running two successful theatre companies. *Some Achieve Greatness* presents invaluable lessons to help us navigate this unpredictable time.

'Some are born great, some achieve greatness and some have greatness thrust upon 'em.'
WILLIAM SHAKESPEARE, *TWELFTH NIGHT*

www.ingramcontent.com/pod-product-compliance
Lightning Source LLC
Chambersburg PA
CBHW010718300426
44114CB00022B/2889